Leading Ladies

Willing Hearts,
Willing Hands

Teresa Hampton

**Foreword by
Jane McWhorter**

Publishing Designs, Inc.
Huntsville, Alabama

Publishing Designs, Inc.
P. O. Box 3241
Huntsville, Alabama

Third Printing: January 2005

Photograph of author on back cover courtesy
of Bill Malone, Valdosta, Georgia.

Printed in the United States of America

Publisher's Cataloging-in-Publication Data

Hampton, Teresa
Leading ladies: willing hearts, willing hands./Teresa Hampton; foreword
by Jane McWhorter.
126 pp; 21.59 cm.
Thriteen chapters—Teacher Outlines—Questions.
1. Women—Leadership. 2. Christian Life.
I. Hampton, Teresa. II. Title.
ISBN 0-929540-24-7
248.8

To my mother,
Mildred Davidson Chester,
who, as a young bride,
began to lead her family toward God.
Her quiet persistence in faithful worship
eventually led her husband to obey the Lord.
He was just the first of many.
She continues to inspire me daily
to grow as a true servant
of Jesus Christ.

Also to the many women
who have touched my life
with their wisdom, courage, and strength:
my "Aunt" Evelyn Crowell,
Cathy McGaughy,
Pheobie Slocum,
Elaine Teffeteller,
Jane McWhorter,
and so many others
who have shown leadership
in its purest form!

CONTENTS

Women have always had a very special place in the Lord's work. The threads of God-ordained male spiritual leadership run throughout the Bible, as God has continually set divine parameters during the Patriarchal, Mosaical, and Christian ages. Many discussions relating to woman's role in the work of the church today, however, seem to focus only on the restrictions God has ordained while failing to accentuate the many positive, unquestionable areas of service open to women.

Negative goodness is not good enough. Simply refraining from participating in restricted areas is not pleasing in God's sight. He also wants women who are busy doing what they should do in the kingdom.

More than half the membership in nearly any congregation is composed of females. Most of these women want to use their talents to the glory of God but often lack direction. We need female leadership in the church—women who are willing to lead other women in doing what is pleasing in God's sight.

The tapestry depicting the divine scheme of roles would sorely be lacking in beauty and strength if it were only composed of the needed sturdy threads of male spiritual leadership. The golden strands of feminine talents are intertwined with masculine abilities throughout the pages of inspiration. The tapestry would be lacking both in beauty and in strength without the suitable blending of these contrasting threads.

A man brings his natural strengths and weaknesses to the service of God, and a woman brings hers. She is strong in many areas in which a man is weak, and his strengths stand in sharp contrast to her weaknesses. Together, they constitute a mighty team in the kingdom.

In the writing of this book, Teresa Hampton performs a real act of service for Christian women. In her refreshing literary style, she traces the golden thread of female roles throughout the Scriptures. If women are going to work effectively, they need female leadership. That kind of leadership must be developed if it is to be effective.

I invite you, the reader, to join Teresa in this vital study.

—Jane McWhorter

Chapter One

WHAT LEADERSHIP IS NOT

Then I heard a voice from heaven saying to me, "Write: 'Blessed are the dead who die in the Lord from now on.' 'Yes,' says the Spirit, 'that they may rest from their labors, and their works follow them.'"

—Revelation 14:13

The old country church, nestled in the back roads of Tennessee, was devoid of modern furnishings. Fold-down, wooden seats braced the faithful as they poured out their hearts to the Lord. Funeral-home fans, combatting the sweltering August heat, pushed a cappella choruses heavenward. And God listened. He listened as His people praised Him.

My childhood years of five through about twelve were spent mostly at this little building, because my parents believed if the doors were open we should be there. While the building itself holds many memories, the people are etched into the warmest part of my heart.

One old gentleman loved to lead the singing. He always chose the same three songs and in the same order. As he led me and the others in song he would often look to the rafters as if he were looking right into Heaven. I felt that this man really, personally knew God. I remember that now and smile, especially when I'm singing one of "his" songs during worship.

An elder of the church and his wife, advancing in years, helped each other into the building and you could set your watch by them. Usually he took her arm or elbow and cared for his little bride as if he were handling gold. I can still see them sitting together in the seat that everyone knew was *theirs*. Both led others, he openly and she in quiet but powerful ways.

Another special memory is the sense of family that this small group of people engendered. I called one particular lady "Aunt Evelyn," although she was not in the least related to me. Her husband was another "uncle." Their girls were about ten years older than I, so I looked to them, trying to emulate every hairstyle, fashion, or gesture. I admired their mother, my adopted aunt, who took an active lead in teaching women and children. She made me feel special. But her leadership did not begin and end with the church. You see, she and her husband owned the little store that was positioned a few yards from the church building and her influence was felt in the community at large. This woman, through her example, led my mother to be active in the church and to lead in the community. She also led me.

I can also, in my mind's eye, see my grandmother. She was a widow who had experienced hard times through the depression. She sat uncomfortably in the old seats, but was thrilled to be "meeting with the saints." I remember one time, though, when she wept openly as the preacher spoke of Jesus and His death on the cross. In her home, in her poverty, she was devoted to her grandchildren. With an unreal measure of patience she drew countless pictures of Bible characters. We colored her drawings as she told us stories of the great heroes of old. Many times she drew and spoke to me from her bed. Her memory leads me today.

A young college-aged woman taught my fourth-grade class during Bible school. I shall never forget her courage. We were a handful. One Sunday in particular, she left the little white church building in tears. When my mother found out how we had disrupted the class—and she *always* found out—she made me apologize to the young teacher the following Sunday . . . in front of the entire class! Though many had participated in the crime, I was the only one whose mother had chosen public humiliation as part of the punishment. That morning it was my turn for tears. A year or so later, I received a letter from that teacher in which she commended me for putting on Christ in baptism. I still have that letter.

When you hear the word *leadership,* what words immediately come to mind? Possibly adjectives like strong, capable, busy, energetic, enthusiastic, or attractive. But do these words ever surface: quiet, single, divorced, young, old, or plain? I must admit that I came into the study of leadership having forgotten some of those childhood memories. I had allowed the world to shape my thoughts of a leader.

Are you like me? Do you have some preconceived ideas of leadership, some of which may be true while others may be misconceptions? It is my sincere hope, as we study this important topic, that as women of God, we will take a fresh look at the topic of female leadership which affects literally every aspect of our lives: our homes, the church, and our communities. Perhaps you will, like me, open the doors to your memory closet and reacquaint yourself with characters who have influenced you to lead.

I was first prompted to study this subject deeply because I was asked to speak during a seminar in the lovely state of Colorado. (Nothing makes a person study quite like the anxiety over an upcoming speaking engagement!) Until then, I had given leadership only a cursory examination. Now I was determined to look not only at the lives of biblical female leaders but to biblical male leaders as well. Another goal was to combine precious morsels from God's word with pearls of wisdom gleaned from women and men who daily enrich my life through word or deed. The subject of women's leadership deserved more than a brief look—it deserved an intense study.

So, in preparation for the seminar, and for my own personal enrichment, I began to search diligently, first looking to see what God said concerning this topic, and then looking to what men and women could offer the study. Going to the dictionary, I found that Webster defines leadership as "the office or position of a leader, or the capacity to lead." The definition of *leader,* however, is not so concise. For the purposes of this study, let us define a leader as a guide or conductor.

Several concepts began to grow in my own mind as I drew from twenty-six years as the wife of a minister. I began to jot down my own thoughts in outline form, collect material from other sources, and pass out an informal questionnaire to women of varying ages and stations in life. One idea became apparent early on as I spoke to women. They were very vocal about the prevailing *misconceptions* of leadership. In fact, being honest with myself, I confess that I had some misconceptions as well.

Misconception number one: A good leader must be an extrovert or have an outgoing personality. *Nothing could be further from the truth!* John Maxwell, in his book, *Developing the Leader Within You,* says,

> Sociologists tell us that even the most introverted individual will influence ten thousand other people during his or her lifetime! . . . That means that all of us are leading in some areas, while in other areas we are being led. No one is excluded from being a leader or a follower. Realizing your potential as a leader is your responsibility (page 2).

As I opened God's word, I discovered Peter's intriguing admonition to women who are married to unbelievers. "Wives, likewise, be submissive to your own husbands, that even if some do not obey the word, they, *without a word,* may be won by the conduct of their wives, when they observe your chaste conduct accompanied by fear" (1 Peter 3:1–2). I know of countless quiet servants who faithfully worshiped God, cared for those in need, and lived chaste Christian lives. These virtuous women eventually led their husbands to obey Christ! If a woman has the ability to lead without speaking a word, then obviously leadership is not confined to those who have outgoing personalities. I have found through the years that quiet people make great leaders *if they have a willing heart*. The introvert usually has finely tuned skills, like listening and organization, which greatly benefit the role of a leader. An outgoing talker has her own obstacles to overcome. She may occasionally have trouble controlling her tongue, whereas the quiet person usually measures her words. The more you open your mouth, the greater opportunity you have to insert your foot. Right? Sometimes what may initially be viewed as an advantage, the gift of gab, becomes a hindrance. While an outgoing personality can assist a woman as she leads others, great listening skills may assist the quiet leader. Being an extrovert is not a prerequisite to effective leadership.

Misconception number two: A good leader must have an active, supportive spouse. *Not true!* In reality, many great leaders began in their youth as a single person, taking leadership roles with success. Miriam was young but with courage assisted in the salvation of her baby brother, Moses. Esther's leadership began when she was a young virgin taken as the queen of a heathen king. As will be seen in a later chapter, she became a dynamic leader of the Jews in a foreign land.

The righteous woman Abigail was married to an ill-tempered drunkard named Nabal (1 Samuel 25). When she realized her husband had insulted David, the hero of the Israelites, she went quickly to work providing food for David's starving army. As she approached David she admitted to him that her husband had acted rudely. Her admission quieted his anger. He made note that her wisdom and bravery had kept him from killing her husband. Abigail returned to her husband. The next morning, when she told Nabal what he had done in a drunken stupor, "his heart died within him, and he became like a stone" (verse 37). When David heard of Nabal's untimely demise he took Abigail as his wife!

In addition to being young and single, many women find themselves "single again" following a divorce or the death of their husband. Do these circumstances of life bring a woman's leadership to a close? The answer is simply, only if she chooses not to lead. Some of the most powerful leaders in the church are widows who practice true Christianity by actively teaching others, whether children or adults, coordinating food groups to assist those who are ill or grieving, and preparing flowers to brighten the hearts of the lonely. The list could go on and on. While it is true that having an active, supportive spouse may facilitate the role of female leadership, it is not essential. Young, single, or single again, women have the ability to actively lead others.

Misconception number three: Leadership positions are best suited for those of a particular age; the age varies depending on the person to whom you are talking. *This concept is false!* Leadership positions are suited to any age. A woman may lead effectively as a young person still pursuing an education, as a new bride, as a young mother with babies tugging on her skirt, as a mother with teens, as a woman experiencing an empty nest, as a grandmother, or as a widow.

God's Word is filled with examples of men and women of all ages who led others with success. David, a young man of about seventeen, rose against Goliath. His brothers scorned his youth, saying he should be back with the few sheep. Humbly, David announced that his strength lay not in himself but in the Lord. God gave him the victory! Ridicule may come to the young who desire to lead, but most young people will receive praise for going against the flow in order to lead others. Indeed, the young deliverer David was praised after defeating the giant and is praised today by those who know his story. Additionally, we read of courageous and strong women who held various occupations as they successfully led others, from the virtuous woman's real estate endeavors to Priscilla's tent making. Naomi, an aging widow, brought her daughter-in-law into fellowship with the nation of Israel and became great-great-grandmother to the second king of Israel.

Aside from parenting, the role of grandparents is one of the most influential in the lives of children. Many a grandmother has been responsible for successfully leading a child to know God's will and to obey Him. Sometimes results are not achieved quickly, as seen in the article by Traci Paseur at the close of this chapter. Seeds are planted, however, and God gives the increase. Never underestimate the power of a grandmother.

Teenage girls may lead. Young mothers may lead. Those with an empty nest may lead. Grandmothers may lead. Some of these women may indeed have more time to devote to the more visible leadership positions than others, but all may serve in various ways to the extent of their abilities. The evidence is in. Age is not a factor. However, willingness is a major factor in this commodity called leadership.

Misconception number four: External attributes like beauty and grace make or break a good leader. *False, false, false!* Beauty is used to sell everything today, so why not leadership as well? This is a lie that Satan has used throughout the years and society has bought into it, as my grandmother would say, "lock, stock, and barrel." The Israelites were no exception. They looked around and saw that all the surrounding countries had kings while they merely had an old judge, Samuel. So they went to him and requested a replacement, Samuel's replacement. A king would be a strong presence among the nations, they reasoned. A king would fight their battles! Samuel warned that while a king might do those things, he would also tax them heavily in order to pay his soldiers. He would draft their sons into his armies. He would take their daughters to make his perfumes and to bake. He would take their cattle and lands.

Despite Samuel's warning, the people would not listen and said, "No, but we will have a king over us, that we also may be like all the nations, and that our king may judge us and go out before us and fight our battles" (1 Samuel 8:19–20). God gave the people what they wanted. When the people were presented with their king, they were entranced. He must have been a statuesque fellow as he stood a head taller than all others. The people shouted, "Long live the king!"

The honeymoon did not last long, however. Saul proved to be a disappointment. His strong physique and kingly presence could not mask his lack of character. Samuel was asked by the Lord to anoint a second king and, as he narrowed the choice down to the sons of Jesse, he felt sure that Eliab, the oldest son who looked like a king, must be the one God had chosen. But God told Samuel,

> Do not look at his appearance or at his physical stature, because I have refused him. For the Lord does not see as man sees; for man looks at the outward appearance, but the Lord looks at the heart (1 Samuel 16:7).

The world may desire beauty and grace in those who lead, but we should heed God's warning to Samuel and the Israelites. The package does not make a good leader. Instead of the infamous question, "Who's the fairest of them all?" women who desire leadership roles should be asking themselves, "Is my heart right with God?"

Opening my mind and heart to the study of leadership, I was drawn to childhood memories of the little white church in the woods. I remembered men and women who led in various ways accordingly to their abilities and strengths. Do you have such recollections as well? Their memory compels me to set aside misconceptions of leadership. Knowledge that comes through the study of God's Word compels me to discard the worldly "shape" of leadership.

A good leader does not have to be an extrovert or have an outgoing personality. I remember the gentleman who led singing as he looked upward and the little old lady who quietly served as an elder's wife. Quiet individuals make great leaders if they have a willing heart.

With or without a spouse—young, single, or single again—women have the ability to actively lead others. I remember my adopted aunt and her ready heart, eager to serve in the church and in the community. Willingness is a major factor in the ability to lead others.

Leadership positions are suited for those of any age. I remember my widowed grandmother who steadfastly worshiped, although in poor health, and taught her grandchildren even on days when she was bedridden. Just as John the revelator wrote about those who die in the Lord, her works of leadership follow her—they do not die with her (Revelation 14:13).

Finally, I am reminded that though the world may choose a certain type of leader, one that looks the part, a true leader may emerge from a young shepherd boy, or from a frightened young woman who has taken on her first Bible class. While the world has this strange love/hate fascination and preoccupation with beauty, God is always looking for individuals with pure hearts who are willing to lead.

Where Have the Grandmothers Gone?
(Traci Paseur)

The year 2000 is now twenty-four days old. What modern times we live in . . . and my, how these times have changed. I have a birthday approaching and my age is so very insignificant. It doesn't matter because times have changed and I find it discouraging.

I was raised in the church and am so very grateful that my grandmother made a way of life for me. Sunday mornings, Sunday nights, and Wednesday nights were for worship. No questions asked. As a child, I willingly admit to that burst of excitement if for one reason or another we didn't go to church. But for the most part, my childhood days of worship were happy times and I felt the comfort of God's word even then. Sunday afternoons were spent around the dinner table enjoying a wonderful meal that my grandmother had prepared. During those days, you didn't dare take a bite until the blessing was said. I've seen my grandmother give thanks over a bowl of beans and a piece of cornbread. Where have the blessings gone? I ask because I don't know. Maybe we don't want to offend anyone by offering a blessing and we don't want to embarrass ourselves shamefully by doing the honor of giving thanks. We should give thanks that we even have the opportunity to give thanks.

I just can't remember a day that I spent with my grandmother when she didn't refer to God and His glory. I remember, not so long ago, driving with my grandmother on a beautiful fall afternoon. The leaves were turning their beautiful shades of orange and red and my grandmother said, "Only God can make a tree." Of course, I had noticed the fall colors but paid attention instead to my needs, my schedule, and basically, my life. My life at that time had absolutely no room for or any need to be mindful of "God's trees."

On a similar outing on a spring day she began to admire the big white fluffy clouds in the sky. She commented on how beautiful they were and that they "looked like you could sit on top of them and let your feet hang off." I can still hear those words, but the daily commute to punch the time clock has created tunnel vision that blocks out God's wonders. Where has the appreciation of God's beauty gone? Again, I ask because I don't know. Perhaps the drive to be there and get it done has blinded us so much that we don't allow ourselves the moments to remember just how small we are in God's beautiful universe.

My yesterdays are filled with God, His blessings, and a good map with clear directions to His door. My today is filled with anguish over the fact that I didn't lose the map, but intentionally put it away in favor of going my own way. My own way, which has left me lost and without purpose. My tomorrow, I pray, will be filled with hope and reassurance from God that I may take up His map and make my journey through life on the right path. Thanks to my grandmother, I know how to read a map.

Growing up, I can remember my grandmother making us turn away from the television when a beer commercial came on. In recent days, watching anything on television with my grandmother has just gotten to the point that I become embarrassed and fearful of what she might see simply because you just never know what's coming. Today's world needs grandmothers. Someone to speak openly about God and someone to remind us continually of His plan for us and to remind us of His blessings.

So now I ask, "Where have all the grandmothers gone?" I'm just not sure. I do know that my grandmother has started her journey home. Just a few more hours and her work here will be done. Soon, there will be one less grandmother and one less teacher. Thank God for grandmothers who are sent from above. I hope God has a beautiful cloud waiting my grandmother's arrival. One that she can sit on and let her feet hang off. While she's there I hope she will look down at me, through God's trees, and see me reading my map, the map that will lead me to God's door, and hopefully, to a place on the cloud beside her, forever.

—Airport Church of Christ bulletin
Valdosta, Georgia

Questions

1. Do you feel there are misconceptions regarding the role of leadership? Explain.

2. In what ways may an introverted individual lead others?

3. What does 1 Peter 3:1–2 say about a quiet woman?

4. In what ways may a woman lead when she finds herself without an active or supportive spouse?

5. List biblical female leaders who either were not married or did not have a supportive spouse?

6. Describe how young women, as well as those in the middle and aging years, may lead.

7. Describe how the Israelites used outward attributes as criteria in selecting a new leader.

8. What did God tell Samuel with regard to beauty and leadership ability? (See 1 Samuel 16:7.)

9. What additional misconceptions concerning women's leadership come to your mind?

Outline of
"What Leadership Is Not*"*

Introduction: As I remember the little country church in which I worshiped, images of leadership abound. But what about today? Do we allow the world to shape our ideas of leadership? Some women who were questioned about leadership expressed what defines leadership. They were also vocal about what leadership is not.

   I. The first misconception is that a good leader must be an extrovert or have an outgoing personality.

II. Misconception number two is that a good leader must have an active, supportive spouse.

III. The third misconception is that leadership positions are best suited for those of a particular age.

IV. The last misconception is that external attributes like beauty and grace make a good leader.

Conclusion: I was drawn back to the childhood memories of the men and women from my past who led according to their abilities. Their examples reveal that quiet individuals make great leaders if they have a willing heart. We also recognize that with or without a spouse, young or old, and with or without personal responsibilities women have the ability to lead others. Finally, we are taught through scripture that more importance should be placed on the leader's heart rather than her appearance. God is looking for individuals with pure hearts who are willing to lead.

Chapter Two

OIL AND WATER?

When leaders lead in Israel, when the people
willingly offer themselves, bless the Lord!
Hear, O kings! Give ear, O princes! I, even I,
will sing to the Lord; I will sing praise to the
Lord God of Israel.

—song of Deborah, Judges 5:2–3

I find it quite remarkable that one of the great judges of
the Old Testament was a woman—one who lived during a
time when men ruled. The positions of authority and power
were all held by men. But sandwiched between Shamgar
and Gideon is a female judge. A woman! Her name was
Deborah. The people came to her for judgment as she sat
under a palm tree between Ramah and Bethel. She sent for
Barak, of the tribe of Naphtali, and instructed him that the
Lord had commanded him to deploy troops against a cruel
king of Canaan called Jabin. Barak fearfully responded, "If
you will go with me, then I will go, but if you will not go
with me, I will not go!" (Judges 4:8.) It appears Deborah
truly wanted the men to lead, but they were not willing.
She told Barak she would go, but to his shame, God would
"sell Sisera into the hand of a woman." And He did.

As I studied this story of a woman who did not want to
be in control but felt pressed into this position of leadership, I began to wonder about women today. Is it possible to

be a submissive woman as well as a strong, capable female leader in the church? Do women generally not consider their labors to be in the area of leadership? Do most men and women have a very narrow definition of leadership? Because of the command to be submissive to husbands, do women feel they are never in positions of leadership? Are submission and leadership like oil and water, never to be mixed? Or is this simply another misconception of female leadership? I went back to God's Word. I went back to the greatest leader the world has ever known, Jesus Christ.

Sometimes I feel we get a bit confused on the subject of submission when, in fact, the subject is not for females only. Submission is a part of daily life, regardless of gender and age. Children submit to parents and teachers. Teenagers submit to parents—at least that's the goal!—and they begin as young adults to learn submission to civil authorities, which often presents itself as flashing lights in the rear-view mirror. Married women, as emotion-driven creatures, submit to their husbands, the logic-driven creatures (Ephesians 5:22).

Additionally, women, whether married or single, submit to civil authority and to God (James 4:7). Men submit to their employers, to the laws of the land, and to God the Father. Paul told Christian men and women to submit to one another in the fear of God (Ephesians 5:21). Paul also spoke of those who had wholly devoted themselves to the ministry of the saints, and told the brethren to "submit to such and to everyone who works and labors with us" (1 Corinthians 16:16). Peter admonished, "Yes, all of you be submissive to one another, and be clothed with humility. For God resists the proud, but gives grace to the humble. Therefore humble yourselves under the mighty hand of God, that He may exalt you in due time" (1 Peter 5:5–6). The powers that be—governors, presidents, and kings—submit to the Creator, who established ruling authorities among men (Colossians 1:16; 1 Peter 2:13–14). And Jesus Christ, the Son of God, an equal with God, submitted to the Father in the redemption of humankind.

That Jesus was God's submissive Son and at the same time called "God" by God himself, is a difficult thought for human understanding (Hebrews 1:5, 10). The writer of Hebrews continued to quote the book of Psalms:

> You have made Him a little lower than the angels; you have crowned him with glory and honor, and set him over the works of Your hands. You have put all things in subjection under his feet (Hebrews 2:7–8).

Paul encouraged his Philippian brethren to have the submissive mind of Christ.

> Let this mind be in you which was also in Christ Jesus, who, being in the form of God, did not consider it robbery to be equal with God, but made Himself of no reputation, taking the form of a bondservant, and coming in the likeness of men. And being found in appearance as a man, He humbled himself and became obedient to the point of death, even the death of the cross (Philippians 2:5–8).

Submission is obedience, but is not to be confused with blind obedience or blind servitude. Submission flows out of respect, love, and trust—putting your trust in one who mutually loves and serves you and would lay down his life for you. Perhaps that is why, in years gone by, the bride was asked, "Will you love, honor, and obey?"

Do we forget that Jesus came to Gethsemane prostrating Himself before God, pleading with such fervor that His perspiration appeared as blood droplets, "Father, if it is Your will, take this cup away from Me; nevertheless not My will, but Yours, be done"? (Luke 22:42.) Do we forget that His human nature did not desire the ridicule of men, the betrayal of friends, the tearing of His flesh? Jesus learned the huge cost of submission—He "learned obedience by the things which He suffered" (Hebrews 5:8). Submission is obedience.

Jesus, the greatest leader the world has known, practiced submission and gave the best example of such. So, in answer to the earlier question, "Is it possible to be a submissive woman as well as a strong, capable female leader in the church?" Yes! Instead of oil and water, it might more accurately be said that leadership with submission is like cake with icing on top!

The key is finding the correct areas of leadership, those areas that are within divine parameters. In the beginning, even before the fall of man and woman, God established positions of authority—God as the highest authority, man subject to God, and then woman subject to man, "for Adam was formed first, then Eve" (1 Timothy 2:13). God has commanded that husbands are the spiritual leaders of the family, that men shepherd the church of God, and that men serve as deacons in the church. And the Holy Spirit guided Paul to instruct that a woman is not to have authority over a man in spiritual matters (1 Timothy 2:12). But there are many other positions of leadership in which women may serve.

One might ask, "What about Priscilla who, with her husband, taught the great preacher Apollos?" If you study Acts 18:26 you will note that though Priscilla was active in teaching, she did not correct or try to instruct Apollos in the synagogue. Rather, she and Aquila "took him aside and explained to him the way of God more accurately." The teaching was in a very private, one-on-one setting. In other words, Priscilla led within divine parameters!

Women are the workhorses of the church, the backbone! Becoming a capable leader of women is an awesome accomplishment to the glory of God. Becoming a leader and encourager of teachers is an invaluable asset to the church of our Lord. Functioning as an efficient, godly leader in the home as a homemaker, wife, and mother is the most understated position in the world, and yet it is probably the key to healing society's woes. Women are active in evangelism, leading the lost to a precious Savior. Christian female leaders in the community serve not only to accomplish good works, but allow others to see Christ at work in an ungodly world. What an outreach for the Lord and His church! With all the God-given leadership roles a woman possesses, her twenty-four hours a day are spent if she is adequately leading and serving within divine guidelines—there should be no time available to pursue the roles which God intended for men! We see that busyness in the actions of Deborah, whose life was already full to the brim as she tried to quietly lead.

Allow Deborah's leadership to inspire you. Listen to her beautiful song of triumph as recorded in Judges 5,

> When leaders lead in Israel, when the people willingly offer themselves, bless the Lord! Hear, O kings! Give ear, O princes! I, even I, will sing to the Lord; I will sing praise to the Lord God of Israel.

Through her example and the beautiful poetry of her song, readers are made to realize that God always desires followers with willing hearts and willing hands, who are willing to lead.

Questions

1. How did God (through Deborah) respond to the men's lack of leadership?

2. Describe how submission is a part of daily life regardless of gender.

3. Who else must submit to others?

4. What did Paul say about submission between Christians? (1 Corinthians 16:16.)

5. How is submission the same as obedience?

6. How did Jesus, the Son, submit to the Father?

7. What does the life of Priscilla teach women in regard to leadership?

8. In what areas may a woman lead?

9. Describe the conditions of leadership which surrounded the judge Deborah?

10. What three qualities does God desire that His followers possess?

Outline of "Oil and Water?"

Introduction: Deborah gave a beautiful example of female leadership within divine parameters. Being a good female leader does not mean abdicating one's submissive nature.

I. Submission is not for females only. Rather, it is a part of daily life regardless of gender and age.

II. The greatest leader the world has ever known was Jesus Christ and, as an equal with God, He submitted to the Father in the redemptive plan. Submission is obedience.

III. Leadership and submission go hand in hand. Desire leadership within God's plan.

Conclusion: Allow Deborah's leadership to inspire you. Through her example and the beautiful poetry of her song we realize that God always desires followers with willing hearts and willing hands, who are willing to lead.

Chapter Three

AN AGE-OLD TUG-OF-WAR

> Not everyone who says to Me, "Lord, Lord,"
> shall enter the kingdom of heaven, but he who
> does the will of My Father in heaven.
> —Matthew 7:21

It was peaceful. It was perfect. It was Paradise! Only in the mind of God did this place begin to conceptualize. Humankind could never have imagined such a surreal existence. Only in the mind of God germinated the plan to bring a man and woman to life . . . in the Garden of Eden.

The first bump in the road came about not through any design flaw or lapse in judgment by the Creator. In order to create a soul with the ability to think intelligently, to love, honor, and obey, He would of necessity have to create a being with the freedom of choice. Otherwise, the creation would be no more than a wind-up robot. This is not what we would desire in the creation of our own children, and the Father obviously did not desire His creation to be mere robotic toys.

On the contrary, God said,

> Let Us make man in Our image, according to Our likeness; let them have dominion over the fish of the sea, over the birds of the air, and over the cattle, over all the earth and over every creeping thing that creeps on the earth (Genesis 1:26).

The creation known as man and woman came with instructions provided by the designer and the manufacturer. As long as the human "machine" operated according to the designer's specifications, he/she operated smoothly. The designer knew the pitfalls of improper use. In fact, He devised a backup plan in case man and woman should, in a moment's folly, discard the instructions (Ephesians 1:4).

Eve was in what some might consider an idyllic situation in the garden. She was able to have children easily without extended pain or sorrow. She never had to worry about meal planning and preparation because everywhere she looked, there were trees filled with ripe, luscious fruit. Wrinkles? No problem. Skin and muscles going south with age? No problem. She had no concern about graying hair, creaky joints, or loss of energy. After all, this was Paradise with its own fountain of youth called the tree of life. Yet, when confronted with temptation, deception in its truest form, she threw out the instruction manual, trusted her own desires, her own eyes, and her own wisdom (Genesis 3:6).

In that moment, in a split decision, the world as they knew it underwent a dramatic change, the introduction of an age-old tug-of-war between good and evil which exists even to this day. Adam followed Eve's lead. Scripture reveals that though she was deceived by the crafty serpent, her husband violated God's command with eyes wide open (1 Timothy 2:14). With their choices came consequences— separation from God and His tree of life. No longer could she sail through pregnancy and childbirth. And no longer could she depend on all the accommodations and meals provided in the heavenly resort called Paradise (Genesis 3:16, 24).

One wonders if Eve spent the rest of her life with this question on her lips, "Why did I have to do things my way instead of God's way?" It became a lesson with bitter consequences for humankind and for God Himself. The Father's backup plan went into motion which would, millenniums later, require the sacrifice of His own dear Son (Genesis 3:15).

The lesson which virtually shouts from the Genesis account is that men or women, it matters not the gender, experience disaster when they set about to follow their own instructions, disregarding God's will. When a woman seeks to successfully lead her family as a homemaker, lead children through teaching, lead women in the church, or lead others in community efforts, wisdom—wisdom from above —dictates using the owner's manual provided lovingly by the Designer.

Not only did God provide a record of Eve's disastrous attempt to lead, He also gave us numerous accounts of those individuals who stubbornly, selfishly, jealously, or proudly lived life as Frank Sinatra sang, by doing it "my way!" Following the garden incident, we learn of the aging and infertile Sarah and Abraham. God announced there would be a son. But Sarah, beginning to question God, decided to alter the plan somewhat (Genesis 16:2). Abraham agreed to take Sarah's handmaid, Hagar, and a child was conceived, which immediately brought animosity into what had been a cozy family circle (Genesis 16:4). Bitter consequences. Later, according to God's plan and His timetable, Sarah conceived at the age of eighty-nine, giving birth to the rightful heir, Isaac, when she was ninety years old (Genesis 21:1–7).

In his Genesis account Moses continued to reveal the lives of other men and women who decided their way was better than God's way. Mrs. Lot was turned into salt. Bitter consequences. Rebecca encouraged Jacob's participation in a great deception staged in order to ensure his father's blessing (Genesis 27:5–17). Murderous anger filled Esau, which forced Rebecca to send Jacob far north to visit her brother until Esau's temper cooled. Rebecca never saw her favorite son again and Jacob never saw his beloved mother's face after the departure!

Moses' account of these events is reminiscent of the old proverb: What goes around comes around. You see, Jacob found himself on the receiving end of first one deception— when Laban switched daughters at his wedding—and then a second which held such irony. Jacob, who had long ago tricked his blind father in order to receive the blessing, was deceived by his own sons into believing that his favorite child Joseph had been killed by a wild animal. Bitter consequences resulted from the actions of those who were not willing to wait patiently on the Lord, not willing to trust Him, those who took matters in their own hands.

Moses' sister, Miriam, obediently served her mother, resulting in the salvation of her baby brother (Exodus 2:4). At least eighty years later, she led all the women in a glorious song of triumph and praise following the miraculous trek through the Red Sea (Exodus 15:20–21). However, later in the wilderness Miriam, along with Aaron, began to speak against Moses because of the Ethiopian woman he had married. (See Numbers 12:1–15.) She declared that she and brother Aaron were God's spokespersons as well as Moses (Numbers 12:1–2). Her arrogant declaration displeased and angered God. She had a heart that was unwilling to yield to God's will. In stark contrast to Miriam's arrogance, scripture says, "Now the man Moses was very humble, more than all men who were on the face of the earth" (verse 3). Humility has always been a key ingredient in the character of people whom God chooses to work His work. Following Miriam's words of rebuke, she suddenly became leprous, "as white as snow." Bitter consequences. Only after Moses' entreaty with God, and her punishment of being shut out of the camp for seven days, was Miriam restored.

One of the most remarkable leaders of the Old Testament is the first king of Israel—remarkable because he had so much potential, and sad because he lost everything. He was selected by the Lord, but the people were quite pleased with the choice, as if they had made it themselves. Saul was a man's kind of man! Tall (standing a head above others), dark, and handsome, "there was not a more handsome person than he among the children of Israel" (1 Samuel 9:2).

At first he reluctantly accepted this role, as he hid among the equipment when Samuel was proclaiming the identity of the new king. He began as one who desired to do God's will, but his heart began to change as he gained power among the Israelites. Scripture reveals a man whose self-willed heart led him to spare King Agag and the best of the Amalekite sheep, oxen, and lambs, when God had specifically commanded to "utterly destroy all that they have, and do not spare them. But kill both man and woman, infant and nursing child, ox and sheep, camel and donkey" (1 Samuel 15:3).

In contrast to the unwilling heart of King Saul, the Lord saw in David a heart that was willing to yield to His will, and an unmoving faith which sustained him through the years of treachery as Saul continued to spiral downward. Scripture reveals that David could have traveled the same road as Saul. In fact, he was headed down a wicked path of lust, adultery, and murder. The difference between the two leaders appears to be that David, when confronted by Nathan with his sins against Uriah, did not make excuses or try to pass the blame to others. He said simply, "I have sinned against the Lord" (2 Samuel 12:13). He accepted the bitter consequences of his sin and the Lord did not put him to death.

Later in life David wanted to build a permanent structure honoring the Lord, but God revealed to him that he could not do so. Rather, the temple construction would be the responsibility of his son, Solomon. David obediently yielded to God's will, collected the materials, and delegated the job to his son. Leaders today would do well to model the heart of the second king of Israel, one who did not seek his own will, one who readily confessed sin and shortcomings, and one who allowed God to mold him into a powerful influence. David had a willing heart and willing hands, and he was willing to lead!

Fortunately, we also read of others who, like David, chose to follow the Creator's instructions. Were they perfect? Certainly not! One might say most were flawed individuals who grappled with loneliness, materialism, lust, fear, adultery, even murder. Over the course of a hundred-year span of time, Noah endured public rejection as he patiently labored in a divine construction program . . . the building of an ark. Abraham offered his son Isaac. Joseph yielded to God when it might have been more desirable to yield to Mrs. Potiphar. Joshua chose righteousness, not only for himself, but also for his family. Deborah led when men refused to lead. Gideon, at first very reluctant, became a redeemer and judge of Israel.

Moses, after receiving the tablets, was confronted with a leader's worst nightmare—mutiny. The aging leader burned hot with anger as he beheld the golden calf fashioned by his own brother. He cast the tablets down against the foot of the mountain and administered necessary discipline to the unruly Israelites. He again climbed the summit so the Lord might give him the law. Do you remember how Moses appeared to the people as he came down from Mount Sinai the second time? His face shone because he had been in the presence of the true Light.

One of the first steps toward successful leadership in the human realm is asking ourselves this question, "When people draw near us, do they recognize that we know God?" Toward the end of his life, the apostle John so aptly wrote to believers, "Now by this we know that we know Him, if we keep His commandments" (1 John 2:3). A Christian, one who desires to lead others, has a heart that yields to God's will, but you cannot yield to that which you do not know. *If one wants to know God's way, one must know God's Word.* If you find yourself lacking Bible knowledge, become a good Bible student. Increase your understanding of God's will for humankind. Know His Word.

These stories of the faithful and the not-so-faithful serve as strong examples of success and failure in leadership. Take note of Eve's disastrous attempt to lead as she discarded the "instruction booklet." Additionally, remember those who sought to please God before they sought to lead precious souls. If you desire leadership, think about and emulate those women with whom you have touched shoulders through the years who were able to accomplish great things to the glory of God as they yielded to His will.

Immediate, glad obedience to God sets our course on the sea of happiness. Disobedience drops anchor in the sea of despair. Godly living means no regrets about yesterday, no embarrassments today, no schemes for tomorrow. Trust and let the One who holds both the past and future be your Guide for the present.

—Author unknown

Questions

1. Who was the first human being to discard God's instructions?

2. What did she give up when she chose her own way?

3. What great lesson may be gleaned from this Old Testament account?

4. How did Sarah rearrange God's plan? What were the results?

5. How did Rebecca rearrange matters? What were the results?

6. How did Miriam attempt to enforce her will? What were the results?

7. How did King Saul disregard God's will? What were the results?

8. In contrast to Sarah, Miriam, and Rebecca, which characters of the Old Testament attempted, at least most of the time, to do things God's way? What were the results of their obedience?

9. What must one know in order to know God?

Outline of
"An Age-Old Tug-Of-War"

Introduction: Scripture reveals that since the dawn of time men and women experience disaster when they set about to follow their own instructions, disregarding God's will.

I. The Bible is replete with examples and warnings of other leaders who refused to do things God's way and failed miserably, such as Sarah, Mrs. Lot, Rebecca, and Miriam.

II. The Bible contains many examples of those who victoriously led according to God's way, like Noah, Abraham, Joseph, Joshua, Deborah, Gideon, and David.

III. A good leader knows the importance of yielding to God. Moses drew close to God to receive the law. He so intently tried to follow God's plan that when he came down from the mountain, the people knew he had been with God just by looking at his countenance. The leader must ask herself, "Do people recognize that I know God?"

Conclusion: Failure is the result when we choose to do things our own way. If one wants to know God's way, one must know God's word. Become a good Bible student. Increase your understanding of God's will for humankind. Know His word.

Chapter Four

HOW FULL IS YOUR CUP?

I waited patiently for the Lord; and He inclined
to me, and heard my cry. He also brought me
up out of a horrible pit, out of the miry clay,
and set my feet upon a rock, and established
my steps. He has put a new song in my mouth
—Praise to our God; many will see it and fear,
and will trust in the Lord.

—Psalm 40:1–3

As a child, I would often hear it said, "You cannot fill someone else's cup if your own cup is empty." I didn't fully understand what the maxim meant until years later, when as a young minister's wife, I was forced to juggle the leadership of women while going through some difficult personal trials. I came to realize that these dark days began to chip away at my spiritual cup, and leadership roles were increasingly hard to embrace.

There were seven children in my family. I was the second and designated little mother of the household. My entire life had consisted of babies, children, and the joy of children's laughter. When my husband and I decided to begin our family, it never occurred to me that there might be problems associated with fertility. The months and years that followed were not just difficult; they were a nightmare. Finally a doctor courageously told us we would never give birth to our own children.

Looking back, I realize how hard it was for me to function daily with even the simple tasks, but life was complicated further because I wanted to be a good minister's wife, which necessarily entailed leadership positions. I came to realize, however, that I simply could not juggle infertility and leadership at the same time. The people of that kind church did not brow beat me or make me feel guilty for not being more involved, and God, through His divine providence and the avenue of adoption, gave us a son and daughter in four short years. I was able to resume some responsibilities and continued to grow in leadership skills.

More recently, when I was hospitalized with severe vision impairment and paralysis, the diagnosis of multiple sclerosis was a bit earth shaking. Questions immediately floated through my mind: How would I function as a minister's wife with this disease? How would the church react to a minister's wife who might become disabled? Would I still be able to lead others in my own quiet way? Fortunately, the wife of one of our shepherds came to me and recounted her bout with life-threatening cancer. I will never forget Elaine's soft-spoken words of consolation, "If you have to get sick, this church is the best place in the world for understanding and care!" She will probably never know how much hope those words gave me as my husband and I were grappling with the unknown. I thank God for our church family which recognized that at times leaders go through spiritual valleys and need time to refill their cup. With their prayers, their love, the unwavering love of my husband, and the power of the Creator, He has restored my health and again I have been able to resume a measure of leadership positions. God is so good!

The women who completed my questionnaire were consistent in their responses. Each revealed one crucial element needed by women as they commit to lead others—a strong measure of spirituality. These women are holy, pure, devoted to God, and devoted to God's truth. However, there have been times in their lives, as in most people's lives, that their own spirituality resembled the ebb and flow of the tide rather than the constant, mighty rushing river. What happens to a woman's spirituality when she suddenly loses a child in death? What happens to her level of devotion to God when she is told by doctors that she has an incurable disease? What measure of holiness is hers when she faces widowhood and for the first time must make decisions without the comfort and counsel of her best friend? Should she try to continue to lead others in good works as she bears her own burdens. Or, are her leadership days a thing of the past? What is a woman to do when she feels her own spiritual cup has a slow, steady leak?

Leaders must be spiritual to the core, but let us not forget one essential point—they are human. As I turned to God's word to break the inconsistency, scripture revealed that spirituality is not a constant. Several individuals came quickly to mind—Job, Samuel, and Elijah.

Do you remember the human tower of spiritual strength called Job? When readers are first introduced to this man, he seems to have everything of which dreams are made. He is called blameless and upright, one who feared God and ran from evil. He had ten children who were constantly in his prayers; he possessed many riches—seven thousand sheep, three thousand oxen, five hundred donkeys, and a large household. Though we do not know much about Job in leadership positions, it would be safe to assume that he was a remarkable leader within his family, his household, and his community. We are told that Job prayed continually for his sons and daughters, and his servants and friends turned to him loyally during his moments of crisis (Job 1:5; 13–19; 2:11–13).

You know the story. Satan proposed to God that Job was so protected and hedged with his children and riches that he would never be tempted to curse the Almighty. God allowed Satan to have power over all Job's possessions. In one swift move Satan wiped out the oxen and donkeys, the servants, the sheep, the camels, and then horror of horrors, all of Job's children were killed by a great tornadolike wind. Remarkably, Job blessed God instead of cursing Him (Job 1:21). Not to be undone, Satan again approached God, asking for another stab at righteous Job. In his own inimitable, taunting way, he challenged God: "Stretch out Your hand now, and touch his bone and his flesh, and he will surely curse You to Your face!" God allowed Satan to strike Job with painful boils, "from the sole of his foot to the crown of his head" (Job 2:7). Not only did Job have to contend with excruciating pain, he also was forced to contend with his wife who encouraged him to "curse God and die!" Still, scripture says, "Job did not sin with his lips." But we do get a glimpse of the struggle which overcomes one who is going through a physical hardship that, day by day, begins to chip away at one's spiritual integrity.

Friends who came with the intent to console Job, in truth were a source of more pain and confusion. Have you ever, in sheer frustration, wanted to just open the heavens and sit down and have a chat with God, asking all those "why" questions? I've been there. What a wondrous promise Christians have, though, as we are assured that the Holy Spirit takes our inexpressible concerns and makes intercession for us "according to the will of God" (Romans 8:26–28).

If Job desired an audience with God, he got his wish. But answers were not forthcoming. In fact, God told Job, "Now prepare yourself like a man; I will question *you,* and *you shall answer Me.*" And the Creator began to ask a series of unanswerable queries: "Where were you when I laid the foundations of the earth?" "Who determined its measurements?" "Who shut in the sea with doors?" "Have you commanded the morning since your days began?" "Where is the way to the dwelling of light?" "Can you lift up your voice to the clouds, that an abundance of water may cover you?" "Can you send out lightnings, that they may go?" "Have you given the horse strength?" "Does the hawk fly by your wisdom, and spread its wings toward the south?" "Does the eagle mount up at your command?"

The questions went on, and on, and on, until finally God asked Job to answer. Clothed in humility, Job recognized that God "can do everything, and that no purpose of Yours can be withheld from You" (Job 42:2). God knows that men and women go through spiritual valleys, but He desires that we seek Him as we grope in the darkness, "knowing that the testing of your faith produces patience. But let patience have its perfect work, that you may be perfect and complete, lacking nothing" (James 1:3–4). There are very few individuals, if any, who would proclaim they enjoy trials and tribulations. But James reminds us that good comes from adversity. Just as gold is refined by fire, the Christian is refined, or made perfect, by adversity.

The problem most of us face is as old as righteous Job. We tend to get stuck in our own troubles; we let the adversity define our lives; we take our focus off the Creator who is, and always has been, in control of the affairs of men. Job learned this lesson as God questioned him. Even from the beginning, Job had all the right answers, first with his wife, then with the friends who came to comfort. But in his heart he kept asking the question many of us ask when we are going through a dark valley, "Why, Lord?" Perhaps the intense grief, or the pain, caused him to question the Creator. But, you see, when Job remembered that God was in control of all things, his trust in Him was also restored.

A similar pattern appeared in the life of the great Israelite judge and leader, Samuel. How would you feel if, after devoting your entire life to the service of a nation you loved, the people heartlessly said, "We don't want you anymore!" Samuel felt what any leader would feel. Intellectually he knew that the people just wanted to be like "every one else."

(Sound familiar?) He knew they wanted a strong, visual presence as they lived among other nations, and the people thought only a king would provide that kind of aura among men. But Samuel became focused on himself. The people had rejected him.

He went to God, expressing the desires of the people, and God immediately cut to the heart of the problem when He said, "Heed the voice of the people in all that they say to you; for they have not rejected you, but they have rejected Me, that I should not reign over them" (1 Samuel 8:7). Samuel had been letting the situation define him. Instead of "Samuel, Leader of Men," he visualized, "Samuel, Rejected By Men."

God helped Samuel redefine the situation. He directed Samuel to the truth of the matter and then directed him back to the work of the Lord, the process of finding a king for this materially driven nation. He didn't allow Samuel to get stuck in the problem. Later, God helped Samuel in a similar way. One might imagine that the aging judge would rejoice when he saw his replacement—King Saul—make blunder after blunder. Not so! Finally, God told Samuel to deliver the shattering news to the king that God had rejected him as king of Israel (1 Samuel 15:11). Samuel was overtaken in grief and cried all night! His mourning continued, until God came again to him saying,

> How long will you mourn for Saul, seeing I have rejected him from reigning over Israel? Fill your horn with oil, and go; I am sending you to Jesse the Bethlehemite. For I have provided Myself a king among his sons (1 Samuel 16:1).

It took some convincing, but Samuel did as he was commanded.

Elijah's victory on Mount Carmel must have created within the prophet an enormous spiritual high. Talk about a mountaintop experience! Using Elijah as His spokesman, God defeated the fictitious Baal in the contest on the mountaintop, and Elijah executed 450 prophets of Baal. He fol-

lowed the astounding contest with another amazing work
of God, the ending of the long drought (1 Kings 18:20–46).
King Ahab did as he was told by Elijah and ran to Jezreel,
whereupon he immediately recounted to wicked Queen
Jezebel all that the prophet had done. Jezebel took matters in her own hands, as often was the case, and sent word
to Elijah that by the next day he would be as dead as the
prophets he had executed. Elijah ran for his life and eventually hid in a cave near the mountain of God.

The word of the Lord came to him, asking, "What are
you doing here, Elijah?" He told God that he had been very
zealous for the Lord (as if God didn't know this). The reward, he said, for his many courageous acts was that he
was all alone now in the battle against evil and soon they
would take his life (1 Kings 19:9–10). In reality, Elijah was
in the middle of a major pity party. He had convinced himself that all the other righteous men and women had been
put to death, leaving him to play a cat-and-mouse game
with a wicked king and queen. Elijah had had enough of
this leadership business.

A great, strong wind tore into the mountains, then an
earthquake, and after the earthquake a fire. After the fire
came a still, small voice, the voice of God telling Elijah to
anoint Hazael as king over Syria, anoint Jehu as king over
Israel, and anoint Elisha as his replacement. God also revealed to Elijah that in no way was he alone in the battle
between good and evil, saying, "I have reserved seven thousand in Israel, all whose knees have not bowed to Baal,
and every mouth that has not kissed him" (1 Kings 19:18).

With a still, small voice God had forced Elijah to realize he had taken his focus off the Creator and had concentrated on his own woes. God redefined the situation; God
redirected him in the work that had to be completed, gave
him a trusted servant in Elisha, and comforted him with
the knowledge of the many faithful who were continuing
to honor God in Israel.

The resounding lesson for leaders must be that when trials, disappointments, depression, grief, or physical illness draws us away from the work of the Lord, and they will, we must remember that the work of God must go on. If we continually look to God during the difficult moments, He will refill our cup, pointing us back to the positive force which refreshes our souls. If we give Him the opportunity, He will direct us back to the work of the Lord which must go on, as He did with Job, Samuel, and Elijah.

Perhaps David captured the essence of peace and security which many of us experience after going through trials,

> I waited patiently for the Lord; and He inclined to me, and heard my cry. He also brought me up out of a horrible pit, out of the miry clay, and set my feet upon a rock, and established my steps. He has put a new song in my mouth (Psalm 40:1–3).

David praised God and remarked that many will observe God's deliverance, and this observation will cause them to trust in the Almighty.

Don't Quit

When things go wrong, as they sometimes will,
When the road you're trudging seems all up hill,
When the friends are low, and the debts are high.
And you want to smile, but you have to sigh,
When care is pressing you down a bit,
Rest if you must, but don't quit.

Life is strange with its twists and turns,
As every one of us sometimes learns,
And many a failure turns about,
When he might have won had he stuck it out;
Don't give up though the pass seems slow,
You may succeed with another blow.

Success is failure turned inside out,
The silver tint of the clouds of doubt,
And you never can tell how close you are,

It may be near when it seems so far;
So stick to the fight when you're hardest hit,
It's when things seem worse, that you must not quit!

The ability to meet affliction with an uncompromising endurance and unflinching respect for God is one of the marks of true Christian character.

—Author unknown

Questions

1. What is meant by the expression, "You can't fill someone else's cup if your own cup is empty?" Do you agree with this statement?

2. What did God allow Satan to do to Job?

3. Have you ever been in a situation in which you wanted to have an audience with God and ask why? If so, relate your situation.

4. God helped Job to refocus, drawing him away from the adversity in his life, by asking what questions?

5. How do you believe Samuel felt when the people demanded a king?

6. How did God help Samuel to refocus, to refill his cup?

7. What was Elijah's response when he heard that Jezebel was going to kill him?

8. How did God approach Elijah and what did God say to help Elijah redefine the moment?

9. What do you believe David was experiencing as he wrote Psalm 40?

Outline of
"How Full Is Your Cup?"

Introduction: You cannot fill someone else's cup if your own cup is empty. So, how full is your spiritual cup?

I. My own personal struggles with infertility and sudden, life-altering illness have led me to understand that leaders are human. Their doubts and fears are similar to others who experience disappointment, sadness, or other strong emotions of the heart.

II. Spirituality is not a constant. There are times in the lives of leaders when their own spirituality may be shaken by the trials of human existence.

III. Job did not allow adversity to define his life. As leaders, we should not allow adversity to mold us, but let adversity refine us.

IV. Following the devastating rejection Samuel experienced, God helped him redefine the situation by directing him back to the work of the Lord.

V. With a still small voice God forced Elijah to realize he had taken his focus off the Creator and concentrated on his own woes.

Conclusion: Do not assume that if you cannot lead today, you can never lead. Spiritual leaders sometimes have lows, trials, disappointments, depression, grief or physical illness which draws them from the work of the Lord. Continue to look to God, as David wrote, and He will refill your spiritual cup.

Chapter Five

A Servant in Shepherd's Clothing

> I am the good shepherd; and I know My sheep, and am known by My own. As the Father knows Me, even so I know the Father; and I lay down My life for the sheep.
> —John 10:14–15

As mentioned in chapter 1, in order to facilitate this study of female leadership I enlisted the aid of women by means of a brief survey. I typed and made copies of my own questionnaire, in which I asked women of varying ages and stations in life the following question, "What are the important qualities possessed by female leaders in the church?" In addition to the informal survey, I did not restrict my study to books designed for women. In fact, I found few books or articles about leadership dedicated solely to women. I did, however, uncover quite a lot of literature directed toward men and leadership. I quickly realized that many of the basic principles of leadership, written and designed for men, may be applied to women as well.

One theme ran continually through my own notes, the responses to the questionnaires, and the books dedicated to leadership. Each source revealed the importance of service, and many specifically mentioned one who left a perfect pattern for success in leadership, Jesus Christ. Let us continue on the road to great female Christian leadership with a look at One whose examples of leading men and women are timeless, examples from the Master Himself.

Jesus had what some might consider a monumental task—only three short years to guide twelve men of His calling into spiritual maturity, knowing all the while that one man would betray Him, one would deny Him with oaths, and all would forsake Him. But He continued to lead. His statistics are staggering even by today's standards. He delivered at least twenty discourses or sermons; shared at least thirty-one parables; performed at least thirty-five miracles; healed lepers, paralytics, the blind; fed thousands with one small lunch intended for a boy; cast out demons; and raised the dead. The apostle John tells readers that there were many other things Jesus did "which, if they were written one by one, I suppose that even the world itself could not contain the books that would be written" (John 21:25).

Where Jesus went, His disciples followed and observed. They watched the Servant at work and they gained an additional side benefit—they learned how people "tick" and they learned about themselves. Jesus served men, women, children, young, old, sick, and sin-sick. These observations gave the apostles three years to learn about people's idiosyncrasies and their needs, and about their own strengths and weaknesses.

Toward the end of His ministry, just before Passover, He and the twelve congregated in a room for supper (John 13:1–17). Even though Jesus had told them of His impending death on more than one occasion, the apostles were still under the mistaken impression that He was there for one purpose, to establish His kingdom on earth. Their idyllic image had been one of Jesus Christ sitting on His earthly throne as King. He would, after the similitude of victorious King David, rid the land of promise of the filthy, heathen Romans. It logically followed—at least in the minds of some apostles—that He would reward His closest friends, the apostles. As His right-hand men, they would help Him rule the world. Jesus knew that this image was soon to be shattered and He wanted to leave these men with the keys to a correct vision of His kingdom, the church.

Jesus rose slowly from the table, removed His outer garment, picked up a towel, and tucked the end in His belt. Pouring water into a bowl, He began to wash one of the disciple's feet, wiping them dry with the towel at His waist. He moved to the next disciple and repeated the process, and then the next, and the next. That is, until He came to Peter. Eyes wide with shock and dismay, that disciple asked, "Lord, are you washing my feet?" With compassion Jesus said, "What I am doing, you do not understand now, but you will know after this" (John 13:7). Knowing that Jesus, the soon-to-be king, had taken on the task of a lowly slave as He washed and dried feet, Peter declared that he would never allow Him to wash his feet. But Jesus responded, "If I do not wash you, you have no part with Me." I imagine that the dismay on Peter's face turned quickly to cold fear and he answered in his own impetuous way, "Lord not my feet only, but also my hands and my head!"

When the Creator of the universe had finished washing the dusty, dirty feet of twelve puzzled men, He explained why He had performed this humble, servant's act. They recognized Him as Lord and Teacher, and rightly so. He went on to explain that the washing was an example, "If I then, your Lord and Teacher, have washed your feet, you also ought to wash one another's feet."

It is quite natural following the death of a loved one to remember his or her last words and actions. Jesus wanted the twelve leaders to remember the example He left just hours before His crucifixion. He wanted them to understand that the servant spirit is critical to the development of spiritual leaders. Jesus, as the perfect example of leadership, was not afraid to get His hands dirty, quite literally.

If you desire leadership, get to know people by doing the undesirable works that need to be done. Don't ever assume that a lowly job is beneath your dignity. As my grandmother often said, "If you see something that needs to be done, just do it!" That something may be helping a young mother corral her children during worship, or putting out fresh visitor cards. These opportunities will help you understand people and their differences.

Additionally, you will become acquainted with various personality types, communication techniques, and learning styles. Some people are visual learners. That is, they remember visual images more quickly than the spoken word. Others are auditory learners who more readily remember spoken words and like to communicate verbally, rather than through the written word. And there are others who best learn through a multi-sensory experience, such as seeing, hearing, and touching. This knowledge will enable you become a better teacher and leader.

A good listener has the servant-nature of Christ. Learn how to listen to others, instead of always wanting to interject your own life experiences. Listening will enable you to key in on a person's strengths and channel her into a work suited to her.

Looking to the Master, we recognize the importance of serving others and learning about people—their personalities, their pain, their strengths, their weaknesses, and their needs. In the process, we will undoubtedly learn invaluable lessons about ourselves.

Jesus always emphasized the spiritual. He mingled with the poor and the rich, debated law with the elite, told parables to ones eager to know God, and exposed His disciples to every conceivable life situation. He led as a shepherd leads his sheep, modeling the heart of a good shepherd. He became, for all to see and know, a servant . . . in shepherd's clothing.

If you want to rule, learn to serve. If you want to lead, learn to follow. If you want to succeed, learn to make others succeed. The deeper our roots in the soil of service, the more abundant our fruit on the tree of leadership.

—Author unknown

No Small Service

Open up your heart and renew your efforts to serve others. Remember, the small things you do can be a big blessing to others. Here are some things to get you started:

1. Plan with a few friends to take food to a new mother for several days.

2. Send a note of encouragement to the young men who take part in the worship service.

3. Include a widow at your Sunday lunch table.

4. Pick up the laundry of someone who has family in the hospital.

5. Pay a genuine compliment to teenage girls at your congregation.

6. Ask one of the older ladies to share a talent with you.

7. Find out who keeps the baptistry clean or prepares the Lord's supper and thank them. (Sign up to do this good work and be reliable.)

8. Write down when people are baptized and send them a card on their one-year "birthday."

9. Tell a teenager that you appreciate the way he or she listens, sings, or pays attention during worship.

10. Send a note to someone, a month after a family member dies. Remember the year anniversary as well.

11. Go to a new mother's home and baby-sit for her or watch the baby while she reads or rests.

12. Sit with a single mother during worship and help her with the children.

13. Let your children color pictures and send them to shut-ins.

14. Plant flowers at the church building.

15. Pray for someone and tell him/her of your prayer.

16. Make copies of your favorite poem, cartoon, or Bible verse and send them to people who need encouragement.

17. Write to your first Sunday school teacher you can remember and tell her how she influenced your life.

18. Write material for your ladies' class.

19. Write a daily devotional for women and share it with the ladies on Mother's Day.

20. Put to memory fifty-two Bible verses, one for each week of the year, perhaps calling this memory game "Fifty-two Pickup." During each week memorize a new passage, study the context of the verse, and share your thoughts with a friend. These verses will serve as spiritual pickups for you and others.

21. Offer an hour or two each week of tutoring to a child (family) that you know is struggling with academics.

22. Arrange with another young couple to swap baby-sitting. You may use the night out to refresh your marriage, or to visit the hospital (as a couple), or do any number of good works within the church and community.

Additional ideas:

Bigger Horizons

Are you ready to lead groups of two or more? Here are some ideas to get you started:

1. *Flower Groups:* Organize ladies to meet each Wednesday morning to arrange flowers (donated by local florists) in bud vases to deliver to each patient in the nursing home.

2. *I.C.U. Care:* Recruit those who are willing to periodically prepare a platter of sandwiches, individually wrapped cookies, and individually wrapped chips which could be stored in the refrigerator of the waiting room area for family members. The platter has scripture attached with the church's name. (Fruit baskets may serve some areas better. Be sure to check with hospital public relations first.)

3. *Quiet Bags:* Prepare canvas bags (one color for girls, another for boys) containing crayons, a clip-board with several coloring pages, some small quiet toys, and a nutritious snack in a small zip-lock bag (cereal or cheese snacks). The bags are hung on coat hooks in the foyer of the building before the Sunday morning worship. They are changed weekly.

4. *Ladies' Day Out:* Set up a weekly two-hour class for the preschool children of stay-at-home moms. This gives mothers of small children a two-hour break for grocery shopping, etc. Be sure to involve women qualified to care for and teach pre-school children.

5. *Ladies' Night Out:* Recruit twelve ladies, one for each month of the year. Each will plan a theme, spiritual (example: Improving Your Prayer Life) or practical (example: Creating a Memory Book of Thanksgiving Just Past). Next they will plan a place to meet: a home, a restaurant, or some other convenient place. Then

they should plan a time and communicate with the other participants by postcard or church bulletin.

6. *Food Groups:* Organize these groups to care for those who have ill family members or for those who have experienced the loss of a family member.

7. *Monthly Calendar:* List church programs, birthdays, and special events—mailed or distributed monthly. (This program will be greatly expedited by someone who has access to, and is familiar with, a computer.)

8. *Love Bears:* Construct small cotton/fiber filled bears and distribute to a hospital pediatric unit for each child who requires surgery. Sewn into the back is a small patch which says, "Made with Love By Your Friends at _____ Church of Christ."

9. *Baptistry Linens and Nursery Linens:* Coordinate women who will rotate in cleaning and returning items after use.

10. *Teen Devotionals:* Plan and host events for each month of the year. Be sure to consult and coordinate with the youth director to avoid scheduling conflicts.

11. *Lord's Supper Preparation:* Plan weekly or monthly for rotation. Be sure to ask those who will be responsible to complete the preparation for this very important part of worship.

12. *Tuesday Open Bible Study:* Plan and teach a weekly Bible class for women of all faiths. This gives women the opportunity to invite their friends who may worship elsewhere. (Hint: Since this program is evangelistic in nature, begin with a book of the Bible and teach through it. This method will avoid many of the evangelistic pitfalls.)

13. *Resource Room for Bible School Teachers:* Keep the teachers' resource room supplied with appropriate ma-

terials. This opportunity is perfect for the lady who likes to organize. It may require three or four women, depending on the size of the church, to rotate the upkeep of the room.

14. *Bible Class Supervisors:* Plan workshops, train those who have the desire to teach, and select permanent substitutes who can fill in at a moment's notice.

15. *Nursery Supervisor:* Enlist attendants—twelve ladies, one for each month.

16. *Feeding the Flock:* Coordinate and rotate groups that plan and prepare Wednesday evening meals (biweekly or monthly). Charge three dollars per person, with a maximum of ten dollars per family to cover the cost. This may be of great service to families with both parents working outside the home.

17. *Service Skills Class:* Coordinate and teach pre-teen girls and boys about service. Form a "Tabitha Club" and a "Timothy Club" in order to teach basic service skills to pre-teens.

Additional ideas:

Questions

1. Describe how Jesus went about explaining to the apostles the concept of leadership as service.

2. When Peter said no, how did Jesus respond?

3. What was Jesus' explanation for the unusual washing?

4. How important are the following characteristics in the service of leaders:

   a. Knowing and understanding different personality types

   b. Communication techniques

   c. Listening

5. What are some ways in which you can serve?

Outline of
"A Servant in Shepherd's Clothing"

Introduction: A good leader must first be a good follower. The process of service enables one to get to know people, just as a shepherd knows his sheep.

I. As He trained the future leaders, Jesus led the disciples into every conceivable setting. He was a true servant.

II. Jesus, the perfect example of leadership, was not afraid to get His hands dirty as he took up the towel and the washbasin and washed the disciples feet.

III. As you serve, learn communication techniques and listening skills, and study personality types. Learn about yourself as you learn to know others.

Conclusion: Jesus mingled with the rich and the poor, debated law with the elite, told parables to ones eager to know God, and exposed the disciples to every type of situation. Looking to the Master, we recognize the importance of serving others and learning about people. Jesus led as a shepherd leads his sheep.

Chapter Six

EXAMINE YOUR EXCUSES

So the anger of the Lord was kindled against
Moses, and He said "Is not Aaron the Levite
your brother? I know that he can speak well.
And look, he is also coming out to meet you.
When he sees you, he will be glad in his heart.
Now you shall speak to him and put the words
in his mouth. And I will be with your mouth
and with his mouth, and I will teach you what
you shall do."

—Exodus 4:14–15

One of the most memorable events of my childhood was
first being introduced to horseback riding. A friend who
owned horses had invited me to ride one afternoon. I
thought there was nothing to hopping up on a horse and
merrily putting it to a gallop. After all, my friend made it
look so easy. She gave me the lazy horse and she took her
spirited horse.

My first thought was how tall the animal was compared
to me. Then, how powerful the flanks and hooves were compared to my scrawny little legs. Not giving in to sudden,
gut-wrenching fear, I mounted, and off we went down a
dusty path. Soon I discovered that my horse truly was lazy.
He wanted to stop every couple of feet and graze. Connie
kept telling me to nudge him softly with my heels. Occasionally that worked. Finally, tiring of the constant stops, I

thought if a soft nudge made him go a few feet, perhaps a sharp nudge would make him keep up with my friend's frisky mare. Before I knew what had happened, we were at breakneck speed—now I know firsthand what that expression means—and I was grasping the horse's mane or anything else that would keep me above instead of below the animal! Naturally, he headed straight for some very low-limbed trees.

The next thing I remember is Connie telling me to just breathe deeply and think about getting back on the horse as soon as possible. I began to sputter every excuse known to humankind: "The poor horse is winded; let's let him rest!" "He just doesn't like me!" "A person could get hurt trying to have this much fun!" And, "I simply can't get on that beast again!" Connie was persistent and quickly got me up again and riding.

My friend was right. I might never have ridden again if I hadn't swallowed the fear and trusted that I would eventually learn how to feel at ease riding. As I studied the biblical leader Moses, these memories of the first ride on a horse came back to me as a rushing flood. Like me, Moses was a bit confident at first, but after having been thrown, he wasn't quite sure he wanted to ride that horse again! God persuaded him to master this thing called leadership. Two things, fear and excuses, are to be found in his story, as well as mine.

At the young age of forty, Moses had everything on his side. He possessed the strength and vitality of youth—a man in his prime. He had a vested interest in the Hebrew slaves; he was tied to them by birth. And he occupied at least a measure of power as the son of Pharaoh's daughter. Surely the time was right for him to take control and fight for the rights of the afflicted, his brethren. But the time was not right. Moses' premature leap into a role of leadership vaulted him straight into an abyss called failure. He fled Egypt and went to a deserted area where he met a shepherd, Jethro, who had a daughter named Zipporah. Forty years passed as Moses learned how to lead sheep instead of men. Ironically, the sheep probably taught him everything he needed to know about people. You see, without direction sheep will go blindly wherever there is food and water. They do not recognize the threat of a bear or the danger of being near the edge of a cliff. Unlike cattle that are driven in a herd, sheep are led by a shepherd. They know his voice. People and sheep have much in common. The Israelites were a people who went blindly where their lusts led them, not recognizing the threat of sin or the danger of lawlessness. They were like sheep, not wanting to be driven, but willing, at least most of the time, to be led. The forty-year shepherding school in the wilderness did much to prepare Moses for the awesome task of leading God's children.

When Moses had reached the age of eighty, the time was right. God presented Himself from a bush that was burning but not consumed. As the curious Moses drew closer to the strange sight, God called to him from the midst of the bush, commanded him to remove his shoes, and introduced Himself as the "God of your father—the God of Abraham, the God of Isaac, and the God of Jacob" (Exodus 3:6). Moses was afraid and hid his face. God told him that He had seen the oppression of His people in Egypt and He was sending Moses to Pharaoh, that he may bring the Israelites out of Egypt.

The aging shepherd first responded by saying, "Who am I to [do this great deed]?" (Exodus 3:11.) God did not enumerate all of Moses' leadership skills or try to build his self-image, but simply reminded him, "I will certainly be with you." Moses continued, "What shalll I say to them?" (verse 13.) God proceeded to give him the words. Not to be deterred, Moses offered a worst-case scenario, one of those "what if" excuses, "Suppose they will not believe me, or listen to my voice; suppose they say 'the Lord has not appeared to you.'" God answered these concerns by giving Moses three miraculous signs: his shepherd's rod became a serpent, his hand became leprous, and he would be able to turn the river water into blood.

One might think twice about making excuses to the God of the universe, but not Moses. His fourth worry was his inability to speak, "I am not eloquent . . . I am slow of speech and slow of tongue" (Exodus 4:10). At this point, I picture an exasperated Creator. God reminded Moses, by asking a series of questions, that He made his mouth: "Who has made man's mouth? or who makes the mute, the deaf, the seeing, or the blind? Have not I, the Lord?" God did not accept the shepherd's feeble excuses and told him again to go, saying, "I will be with your mouth and teach you what you shall say."

Risking all, Moses, in desperation, said, "Send anybody but me!" (My paraphrase of verse 13.) The anger of the Lord was kindled against Moses and He told him his brother, Aaron, a fine speaker, would be his mouth, God would be with them both, and he would have the miraculous signs. Moses got his house in order and obeyed God's call. Though one would not know it by his fearful beginning, he became a legendary leader and lawgiver.

Generations later, another great leader offered excuses when first asked to lead the army of God. The angel of the Lord addressed Gideon as he sat under a tree: "The Lord is with you, you mighty man of valor!" (Judges 6:12.) One can only imagine that Gideon must have looked around to see if the angel was speaking to someone else. Ignoring the reference to his mighty valor, Gideon delivered a classic "change the subject" excuse. With a bit of sarcasm he asked, "If the Lord was with them, why had He allowed them to be delivered to the Midianites?" Drawing Gideon back to the subject, the angel of the Lord said, "Go in this might of yours and you shall save Israel from the hand of the Midianites." Gideon immediately offered excuse number two. He informed the Lord that He had chosen the wrong person: "How can I save Israel? My clan is the weakest and I am the least in my father's house!"

Even though God assured him that He would be with him, Gideon continued to struggle with unadulterated fear and asked for proof that this was truly God speaking to him. Following the sign, the reluctant leader was still fearful. When the Lord told him to tear down his father's altar to Baal, he obeyed but chose to do it by night because he feared his father's household and the men of the city (Judges 6:27). In the parable of the talents, Jesus spoke of the fear each of us experience when asked to take on a new responsibility (Matthew 25:14–30). The two men who used the talents entrusted to them were praised by the Lord and given more talents. The man who feared and hid his talent was rebuked by his Lord. Fear is not the problem; it is a given. Rather, we should be concerned that fear prompts the correct actions. Gideon continued to test the Lord as twice he put the fleece out at night and checked it the next morning. Somewhat convinced, He called the men to battle.

Gideon's courage must have been bolstered by the astounding number of men, 32,000, who joined him to rise up against the Midianites . . . until the Lord whittled the size down to 300. God reasoned that with great numbers Israel would "claim glory for itself" (Judges 7:2). The Lord told Gideon if he was afraid to go to battle he should take his servant and slip quietly, under cover of darkness, into the enemy camp to do a little eavesdropping. Gideon did just that and led the Israelites as a mighty man of valor!

As I studied the lives of Moses and Gideon, I found at least five kinds of excuses and realized they are not unique to Old Testament times:

- Change the subject: "If the Lord was with them, why had He allowed them to be delivered to the Midianites?"
- Plead insignificance: "I'm not the right person for the job."
- Doubt your abilities: "People won't listen to or follow me."
- Offer a worst-case scenario: "What if the people say, 'The Lord has not appeared to you?'"
- Exaggerate your inadequacies: "I'm not an eloquent speaker."

Jesus addressed the problem of excuses as well as fear, and added a sixth excuse to our list above: "I have too many personal responsibilities." Jesus invited a man: "Follow me," and the man responded, "Lord, I will follow you, but let me first go and bid them farewell who are at my house." Jesus told him, "No one, having put his hand to the plow, and looking back, is fit for the kingdom of God" (Luke 9:57–62). In the parable of the great supper, Jesus told of a certain man who gave a great supper, inviting his friends (Luke 14:16–24). Those who received invitations to the grand affair offered various excuses. The first asked to be excused because he had to see newly purchased land; the second, because he needed to test newly purchased oxen; the third, because he had gotten married. None of those invited were allowed to taste his supper. Instead, the poor, maimed, lame, and blind were brought to the banquet.

Jesus' parables and the remarkable lives of Moses and Gideon reveal that God chose imperfect, sometimes flawed individuals to do marvelous works to His glory. Their examples of fearfulness and excuses should encourage each of us to examine our own reactions when asked to lead. If we respond with fear, we should remember that most leaders experience fear, but learn to overcome with the help of God. If we respond with excuses, we should examine our own words.

Are we any different than these biblical characters when we are asked to lead, if only in a seemingly insignificant position? Do we find ourselves saying: "I'm too young to lead"; "My children require too much of my time"; "With my outside job, there just aren't enough hours in the day"; "There has to be someone more qualified than me": "I'm too old, and besides, I've already served my time"; "If I accept this responsibility, it will be a life-sentence." Do these responses sound familiar?

The lesson that can be gleaned is that mere excuses for not doing the work of the Lord only serves to anger the God of Heaven. He already knows our abilities because He made us. He knows our hearts and the intent of our minds, something we cannot know about each other, so it would be inappropriate to examine the hearts of others (or excuses from the hearts of others). He knows when we try and fail, when we try to ride and fall off the horse. He empowers us with courage to get back on the beast.

When you are asked to lead, remember that fear is a normal response. Fight the urge to give quick excuses. And if you believe you have a legitimate reason which prompts you to decline to lead, remember it is the responsibility of each person to examine herself/himself and ask, "Would I pass the excuse test if Jesus were present to know my abilities and my heart?" And, in fact, as He told Moses and Gideon, He is always with us.

> *Did* is a word of achievement.
> *Don't* is a word of retreat.
> *Might* is a word of bereavement.
> *Can't* is a word of defeat.
> *Ought* is a word of duty.
> *Try* is a word of each hour.
> *Will* is a world of beauty,
> *Can* is a word of power.
>
> —from Ann Landers

Make A Big Difference

Did you ever have the feeling that YOU really didn't
count?
That your ONE vote didn't matter when they totaled
the amount?
Were you sure no one was listening when you wanted
to be heard?
That you couldn't change the current with the wis-
dom of ONE word?
Well, ONE person makes a difference in your family
history
'Cause if ONE and ONE did not make two, they never
could make three!
If you think YOUR views unvalued when the group is
starting goals—
Or the way YOU stamp your ballot isn't worth much
at the polls,
Just remember how mathematics always starts you
out with naught.
And if you don't add ONE unit—then a zero's what
you've got!
It is from only one acorn that the mighty oak tree grows—
And ONE small but sturdy pebble got Goliath in the
nose!
Yes, it does take two to tango—but you need ONE to
suggest.
And perhaps ONE more right answer means you pass
or fail a test.
So the ONE that makes the difference more than often could be YOU.
And it's not just "wishful thinking" but the things
you say and do!
There's a "U" in contribution . . . make it stand out in
a crowd!
'Cause it's EVERY ONE we count on to make our Sav-
ior proud.

Questions

1. Relate an event in your life in which you had to swallow your fear and accomplish what appeared too difficult.

2. What was the outcome of Moses' first attempt at leadership? (Hint: He was forty years of age.)

3. When God approached Moses to lead His people, what excuses did Moses offer?

4. What were Gideon's excuses?

5. What are some commonly heard excuses for not accepting leadership roles?

6. Take a moment and examine your own excuses for not accepting leadership positions.

Outline of "Examine Your Excuses"

Introduction: My first ride on a horse was bit like Moses' first attempt at leadership. I was confident at the beginning, but after having been thrown, I was not quite sure I wanted to ride that horse again. Two things, fear and excuses, are to be found in both of our stories.

I. Moses, when called to lead, offered five excuses.

A. Moses asked the Lord, "Who am I?"

B. His next question was, "What will I say?"

C. Then Moses asked, "What if they do not believe me?"

D. Moses questioned his own abilities when he said, "I am not a good speaker."

    E. Finally, in desperation, Moses said to the Lord, "Send anyone but me!"

  II. Gideon, too, offered excuses when asked by the Lord to lead the Israelites.

    A. His first response to the angel of the Lord was to say, "If the Lord was with them, why had He allowed them to be delivered to the Midianites?"

    B. When the angel of the Lord continued to press Gideon into action, he responded with, "How can I save Israel? My clan is the weakest and I am the least in my father's house!"

  III. Moses and Gideon offered five classic excuses and the Lord dealt with a sixth.

    A. The first excuse was to change the subject.

    B. Next, Moses and Gideon pled insignificance.

    C. Both men doubted their own abilities.

    D. Moses offered a worst-case scenario.

    E. Moses and Gideon exaggerated their inadequacies.

    F. A sixth excuse, having too many personal responsibilities, is revealed in the New Testament as a man responded to Jesus' request, "Follow me." The man replied, "First let me go and bid them farewell who are at my house."

Conclusion: We are no different than Moses and Gideon if we offer excuses for not leading others. Remember that fear is a normal response. Fight the urge to give quick excuses. And if you believe you have a legitimate reason which prompts you to decline to lead, recall that it is the responsibility of each person to examine his or her own excuses. Ask yourself, "Would I pass the excuse test if Jesus were present to know my abilities and my heart?"

Chapter Seven

ACCENTUATE THE POSITIVE

Rejoice in the Lord always. Again I will say, rejoice! Let your gentleness be known to all men. The Lord is at hand. Be anxious for nothing, but in everything by prayer and supplication, with thanksgiving, let your requests be made known to God; and the peace of God, which surpasses all understanding, will guard your hearts and minds through Christ Jesus.

—Philippians 4:4–7

Through the years, as I have worked with many strong, capable female leaders, it has come to my attention that these ladies, without fail, possess an enormous confidence in God. The confidence in Him produces confidence in themselves. They possess an attitude of hopefulness. Again, God gives them eternal hope, and in doing so, He produces hope in all areas of their lives. Their positive nature is contagious. They have the ability to reframe an event, a person, or a situation so they can remain positive in their focus and their ability to lead others in a positive direction.

At first it may sound like these women are superhuman, but each would vehemently deny that presumption. In reality, many would readily admit they had to learn to put aside some very negative characteristics, such as complaining, worrying, or gossiping. They had to learn to be positive in all things, seeing good even in adversity. This is, in a nutshell, the definition of reframing in reference to how we view life and how we view the people with whom we daily rub shoulders.

In the responses to my questionnaire, the characteristic of positivity was repeatedly mentioned as an essential ingredient of leadership. Each woman, as she listed qualities of a good female leader, drew me back to the One who is our model of leadership, Jesus Christ. Throughout His ministry Jesus taught that we could and should reframe the events in our lives. Instead of feeling downcast when persecuted, He said you are blessed and should rejoice (Matthew 5:10–12). If someone compels you to go one mile, go with him two (Matthew 5:41). Instead of hating your enemy, love and bless him (Matthew 5:44). Instead of seeking revenge, forgive. And just as surely as you forgive, your Father in Heaven will forgive you (Matthew 6:12).

All these positive emotions of the heart put a different frame—one of beauty—around what had been an ugly, negative event in our lives. The entire picture, the way we see ourselves and others, has been transformed. People want to be near us, to be near that kind of inner peace. This attitude of hopefulness draws people to follow a great leader, just as men and women were drawn to this man called Jesus of Nazareth. Ralph Waldo Emerson wrote, "Happiness is a perfume you cannot pour on others without getting a few drops on yourself."

As I reflected on Jesus' life, I didn't see a Savior who was in the habit of complaining, worrying, or gossiping. Rather, He was very often found in the company of some pretty negative individuals, men who seemed to thrive on their own complaints and criticism of others. In fact, as I studied how many times Jesus confronted complaints and criticism, I was in awe of the restraint that was shown by our Lord. You see, unlike every other human, He could read their hearts and know their intent. He knew when their complaints were born of jealousy, hatred, misunderstanding, or fear of the loss of power. He showed miraculous restraint as He responded to the whiners of His generation.

Early in His ministry Jesus faced Jews who criticized Him because He said, "I am the bread which came down from heaven" (John 6:41). They reasoned that this man was the little boy known to all as the son of Joseph and Mary, so how could He go around telling folks He came down from Heaven? Jesus reminded them of their ancestors who ate manna in the wilderness, and died. He said, "I am the living bread which came down from heaven. If anyone eats of this bread, he will live forever; and the bread that I shall give is My flesh, which I shall give for the life of the world" (John 6:51).

Despite His words of hope, they continued to quarrel, refusing to open their hearts and minds to the One who offered eternal life. John went on to reveal that even some of His disciples did not understand when they heard His teaching concerning eating His flesh and drinking His blood. They complained about this and from that time "many of His disciples went back and walked with Him no more" (John 6:66).

Jesus faced the complaints of the Pharisees and scribes as they murmured (Luke 5:30; 15:2). They complained that Jesus ate with a sinner, but Jesus calmly assured Zacchaeus in their presence, "Today salvation has come to this house, because he also is a son of Abraham; for the Son of Man has come to seek and to save that which was lost" (Luke 19:9–10).

Jesus, our model of leadership, saw good or the potential for good in all people, even the most reprobate. He saw that a tax collector could become a gospel writer (Matthew), a fisherman could be transformed into a preacher (James), a sinful woman could anoint a King, a doubter could see and believe (Thomas), a loose cannon could introduce the Gentiles to a risen Lord (Peter in the house of Cornelius), and a murderer could travel the world telling the old, old story (Saul of Tarsus).

In His sermon on the mountain, Jesus pointed believers toward a positive outlook in life, a different type of thinking, as He asked,

> Which of you by worrying can add one cubit to his stature? So why do you worry about clothing? Consider the lilies of the field, how they grow: they neither toil nor spin; and yet I say to you that even Solomon in all his glory was not arrayed like one of these. Now if God so clothes the grass of the field, which today is, and tomorrow is thrown into the oven, will He not much more clothe you, O you of little faith? (Matthew 6:27–30.)

Inspired by the Holy Spirit, Paul continued Jesus' teaching about worry when he wrote the Philippian brethren,

> Be anxious over nothing, but in everything by prayer and supplication, with thanksgiving, let your requests be made known to God; and the peace of God, which surpasses all understanding, will guard your hearts and minds through Christ Jesus (Philippians 4:6–7).

The very act of worrying is a waste of precious time and energy.

> Worry never climbed a hill;
> Worry never paid a bill.
> Worry never dried a tear;
> Worry never calmed a fear.
> Worry never darned a heel;
> Worry never cooked a meal.
> Worry never led a horse to water;
> Worry never done a thing you'd think it oughta!

In Philippians 4, Paul advised believers to guard their thinking—meditate on things that are true, noble, just, lovely, of good report, with the promise again that the person who keeps this mind of Christ will have the peace of God. This is the type of leader that attracts followers.

As a woman desiring to lead others, I should ask myself certain questions: Do I find myself worrying about things, or do I trust God in prayer? Am I constantly focused on the misdeeds of others, or do I try to see the good in other individuals, even the cantankerous ones? Am I critical of others and find myself caught up in gossip, or do I try to make others feel good about themselves and other individuals? Am I a whiner, a complainer, a grumbler, or do I use my time and energy in doing good and thanking God for His unspeakable gift? J. Vernon Jacobs, in his book, *10 Steps to Leadership*, says,

Followers desire a leader who is agreeable, and of whom they can be proud. They do not want Fred B., who throws a tantrum every time he cannot have his way . . . They cannot trust Henry M. [or Henrietta], who tells things which are not true, and has the reputation of not being too honest . . . Such things are repugnant to most people and must be replaced with positive qualities which are attractive.

A negative person repels others, but just as honey draws bees, a positive individual attracts others who desire to work with her toward a common goal. A kicking mule doesn't pull, and a pulling mule doesn't kick. If you desire to lead others, set some goals today. Make a commitment that you will be less critical and encourage others to be less critical. Worries, complaints, and criticism serve only to stagnate the work of the Lord. Decide today that you will accentuate the positive.

A Sure Way to a Happy Day

Happiness is
something we create in our minds,
It's not something you search for and seldom find—
It's just waking up and beginning the day
By counting our blessings and kneeling to pray—
It's giving up thoughts that breed discontent
And accepting what comes as a "gift heaven-sent"—
It's giving up wishing for things we have not
And making the best of whatever we've got.

"Happiness consists in activity; it is a running stream, and not a stagnant pool."

"Laughter is the sun that drives winter from the human race."

"Happiness is what greases the axles of the world; don't go through life creaking!"

"Happiness is like potato salad; when you share it with others, it's a picnic."

Garden of Happiness

First, plant five rows of *peas*:
Prayer
Perseverance
Politeness
Promptness
Purity

Next, plant three rows of *squash*:
Squash gossip
Squash doubt
Squash indifference

Then, plant five rows of *lettuce*:
Let us be faithful to duty
Let us be unselfish
Let us be gentle
Let us follow wisdom
Let us love our neighbor

And no garden is complete without *turnips*:
Turn up at meetings
Turn up with a smile!

Questions

1. Describe how a positive outlook aids one who desires to lead others?

2. How did Jesus react to the negativity that surrounded Him?

3. How did Jesus view the following individuals:
   a. The tax collector, Matthew?
   b. The fisherman, James?
   c. The sinful woman who anointed Him?
   d. The doubter, Thomas?
   e. The "loose cannon" called Simon Peter?
   f. The murderer, Saul?

4. How does worry contribute to negative thinking? What did Jesus say about worrying?

5. What are some of the effects of being around individuals who are prone to whine, complain, worry, or grumble?

Outline of
"Accentuate the Positive"

Introduction: Be positive in all things. Put aside complaining, worrying, and negative thinking. See the good even in adversity. Practice this principle while following, so the positive attitude becomes second nature when occupying a leadership position.

 I. Jesus, our model of leadership, saw the good in all people: Matthew, James, a sinful woman, Thomas, Peter, and Saul of Tarsus.

 II. In His sermon on the mount, Jesus addressed the value of having a positive outlook in life when He asked, "Which one of you by worrying can add one cubit to his stature?"

III. Paul continued these teachings about worry when he told the Philippian brethren, "Be anxious over nothing."

Conclusion: A negative person repels others, but just as honey draws bees, a positive individual attracts those who desire to work toward a common goal. If you desire to lead others, set some goals today. Make a commitment that you will be less critical. Also, encourage others to be less critical.

Chapter Eight

GIVE THEM A TARGET

Go therefore and make disciples of all the nations, baptizing them in the name of the Father and of the Son and of the Holy Spirit,
teaching them to observe all things that I have
commanded you; and lo, I am with you always,
even to the end of the age.

—Matthew 28:19–20

Growing up in the country with six brothers and sisters, older and younger, created lasting memories. God's
beautiful creation became an integral part of everyday life.
At autumn time we furiously raked the fallen leaves into
monster piles, not necessarily for the beautification of our
lawn, but to dive madly into our crunchy lake! We plodded
through snow-covered meadows to chop down our Christ-
mas tree. During sultry summer evenings we took clear jars
into the darkness of night and caught fireflies, which at
bedtime became our personal nightlight.

On lazy afternoons during my early teen years, my older
brother, Vick, would take me with him as he practiced with
his hunting bow. He meticulously set a target off in the distance and then began to practice. Placing the arrow in the
bow, he drew it back until the line was so taut I thought it
would break. Taking careful, steady aim, he let it loose.
Swoosh! His arrow hit the red dot in the center. Occasionally, he would encourage me to practice with him. He was a

patient teacher. I learned the importance of having a target out in the distance at which to aim, and of course, I didn't just try to hit the edge of the target. I took steady aim at the red dot. There was such a feeling of grand accomplishment when I hit the bull's eye, or at least came close.

As I recalled this childhood memory, I wondered what would happen if an archer had no target at which to aim. What would happen if a man went into the woods to hunt, bow and arrow in hand—any weapon would suffice—but could never decide which animal to bag. A person simply has to have a target, a goal, a mission statement, a dream, a vision of what she/he wants to accomplish, or nothing lasting will be realized. I wonder if God looks down upon His creation, women and men, and sees us wandering around, doing many things, caught up in busy work. But while we are very, very busy, is it possible we fail to recognize that what we really need is a vision, a purpose greater than life itself?

Joshua, a leader of God's nation, knew the importance of setting before the people a worthy purpose (Joshua 24:15). This man had seen a lot and evidently learned from what he observed. As a younger follower, one who had traveled with the thousands as they fled Egypt, Joshua witnessed a work in progress, the metamorphosis of a nation.

The suffocating, constraining cocoon for the Israelites had been Egypt. When the time was right, God brought them from that land under the leadership of the humble shepherd, Moses. Like a butterfly who had just shed its cocoon, still weak and only beginning to test its wings, the Israelites emerged a weak people—very materialistic, very self-motivated, continually vacillating between the gods of Egypt and the one true God of heaven and earth.

Moses, under the direction of the Lord, gave these people a vision of a life that could be theirs. He made them believe they could possess the land of milk and honey, the land promised long ago to Abraham. He gave them a target. And he showed them the means by which they could reach their land—an obedient relationship with God. He empowered them with strength through the giving of God's Word and taught them how to fly. But not without a few premature crashes, which the young leader Joshua was present to observe.

As they neared the precious promised land, Moses chose a man from each tribe of Israel (Numbers 13:1–25). One of those chosen was Joshua. Moses sent the twelve men into the land to scout, to spy. They returned and gave reports. Ten spies said the land was just as God had described, a land flowing with milk and honey, but the people who inhabited the land were giants compared to Israelite men (verses 26–29). Their negative report struck fear in the hearts of the people.

Stepping forward, Joshua and Caleb said everything was just as the other ten spies had reported, but Joshua added,

> If the Lord delights in us, then He will bring us into this land and give it to us . . . Only do not rebel against the Lord, nor fear the people of the land, for they are our bread; their protection has departed from them, and the Lord is with us. Do not fear them (Numbers 14:8–9).

Joshua took this fearful situation and reframed it. Instead of the giants eating them as if they were grasshoppers, the giant Canaanites would be bread for the Israelites. They had false powerless gods offering them no protection, while the Lord was with the Hebrews.

The Israelite's reaction to the conflicting reports was to call for stones that they might put Joshua and Caleb to death (Numbers 14:10). The ten spies' negative report had succeeded in diverting their attention from the heavenly purpose. They had taken their eyes off the prize. And even though Caleb and Joshua tried to reason with them, the rosy picture of dwelling in a land flowing with milk and honey had been shattered. However, God knew—and His faithful ones knew—that the Israelites themselves were the instrument which had shattered their dream. God said to Moses, "How long will these people reject Me? And how long will they not believe Me, with all the signs which I have performed among them?" (Numbers 14:11.)

Joshua witnessed the punishment of the unfaithful. God said they would never enter the promised land, but their carcasses would fall in the wilderness, "from twenty years old and above. Except for Caleb . . . and Joshua . . . But your little ones, whom you said would be victims, I will bring in, and they shall know the land which you have despised" (Numbers 14:29–31).

The ten spies were struck with a plague and died. And the Israelites were forced to wander in the wilderness for forty years, one year for every day the spies had spent scouting the land. Moses died and Joshua became the new leader. He led the now-adult children victoriously into battle, conquering great, fortified cities. They took the land promised to them centuries before. In time, the people settled, each tribe taking a portion of land, but the mission was not complete.

At the end of the book of Joshua, the aging leader called all Israel together and reminded them what God had done to all the nations around them. Advanced in years, Joshua called to remembrance all God had done for them. He then offered a stirring challenge, saying God has

> given you a land for which you did not labor, and cities which you did not build . . . you eat of the vineyards and olive groves which you did not plant. Now therefore, fear the Lord, serve Him in sincerity and in truth, and put away the gods which your fathers served on the other side of the River and in Egypt. Serve the Lord! And if it seems evil to you to serve the Lord, chose for yourselves this day whom you will serve, whether the gods which your fathers served . . . or the gods of the Amorites . . . but as for me and my house, we will serve the Lord (Joshua 24:13–15).

Nearing death, Joshua drew these people back toward their mission, the vision that God intended for His people, serving the Lord. After these things, he died at the age of one hundred and ten years old (Joshua 24:29). Joshua, one of the mightiest of the great biblical leaders, constantly put God's vision before himself and the people, showing just how important this single act can be as one tries to lead others.

Jesus, the Master, left a pattern of this characteristic of leadership as He gave us a target, a dream, a vision, a purpose. Just as the Israelites remembered Joshua's last words, we remember Jesus' last words before He was caught up in the clouds:

> Go therefore and make disciples of all the nations, baptizing them in the name of the Father, and of the Son and of the Holy Spirit, teaching them to observe all things that I have commanded you; and lo, I am with you always, even to the end of the age (Matthew 28:19–20).

In these few words, He gave each of His followers a target, a purpose greater than life itself.

Jesus' disciples continued to do the same. Having come to a greater understanding of God's purpose after the resurrection, the bold one, Simon Peter, delivered a stirring message on Pentecost: "Repent, and let every one of you be baptized in the name of Jesus Christ for the remission of sins; and you shall receive the gift of the Holy Spirit" (Acts 2:38). On that day thousands were made to realize a greater purpose.

Do you recall the brief life and dying words of the martyr Stephen? He was trying to show a more perfect way to a people whose hearts were stone. Needless to say, he did not have the same response that Peter received on Pentecost (Acts 7). Seeds were planted, however, in the hearts of some, in particular, Saul of Tarsus. Not many days following the stoning of Stephen, Saul journeyed toward Damascus with the sole intent of imprisoning Christians. In a miraculous display of divine glory, Jesus introduced Himself to Saul as he traveled. During his blinding experience on the road, Saul was able to see many spiritual truths and, a few days later, became a Christian. Later called Paul, he began to share God's dream with others, especially those of Gentile persuasion. He spoke to common men and women as well as dignitaries and governors. While at Rome and under house arrest, "Paul dwelt two whole years in his own rented house, and received all who came to him, preaching the kingdom of God and teaching the things which concern the Lord Jesus Christ with all confidence, no one forbidding him" (Acts 28:30–31). The great leaders of New Testament times—Peter, Stephen, Paul, and many others—were constantly emphasizing the dream, a spiritual purpose.

As a Christian female leader in the church of our Lord, I should draw God's people back to our intended purpose, which is (in condensed form), obey God, make disciples of others, and receive the rewards belonging to the righteous. Programs and classes should be periodically evaluated, asking these questions: "Does this good work encourage others to obey God and/or encourage the lost to seek Christ?" "Does this work seek to edify or teach, or are we focusing on entertaining ourselves, satisfying our own demands?" As a school teacher, the question I am constantly asking myself is, "Will this activity help the students reach the required objectives for this course?" The Lord's work should be given the same serious consideration and thought. Every program, every class, every good work (including the daily labors in our homes and community), everything we try to accomplish as a Christian should have as its ultimate goal this mission presented to us by the Savior.

As a leader, help women to set attainable goals or steps, so they might realize that which is everlasting. Keep the target before them, and before yourself. As a leader, continue to seek God's will, seek that which is spiritual, keep a positive outlook, and continue to serve. The writer of Hebrews pictured our Christian life as a race; the intended target was the finish line. He encouraged those of us who are running the race to "strengthen the hands which hang down, and the feeble knees, and make straight paths for your feet, so that what is lame may not be dislocated, but rather be healed" (Hebrews 12:12). If you desire leadership as a Christian woman within divine guidelines, you desire a good thing. Try to gently bring others to remember God's vision for humankind, a target given to us by the Master. There will always be distractions; there will always be those who, like the ten spies, try to evoke fear, jealousy, covetousness, or other diversions which make us forget our target. So as leaders we must do as Joshua, Jesus Christ, and His disciples did; we must continue to point ourselves and others toward the intended target, our promised land which is Heaven.

Quotes

I was taught to think about mission and people. Mission. What are you trying to accomplish? Don't do anything until you know what the mission is. Drilled into our hearts and into our heads.

—General Colin Powell

Not much happens without a dream. And for something to happen there must be a great dream. Behind every great achievement is a dreamer of great dreams. Much more than a dreamer is required to bring it to reality; but the dream must be there first.

—Author unknown,
from *To Dream Again*, by Robert D. Dale

The most pathetic person in the world is someone who has sight, but has no vision.

—Helen Keller

Questions

1. What type of distractions did the Israelites face in the wilderness?

2. How did Joshua give the Israelites a target?

3. What vision or target did Jesus leave all of His followers?

4. How did Stephen direct people?

5. How did the apostle Paul direct people?

6. Evaluate the activities in which you are involved. Ask yourself, "will this activity help others reach our target destination, heaven?"

7. What are some distractions faced by Christians today, those things which make us lose sight of our target?

Outline of
"Give Them a Target"

Introduction: As a child, I used to practice shooting with my brother's bow and arrow. There was such a sense of accomplishment when I hit the bull's eye, or at least came close. Even the simple tasks of life usually require a target, a goal, a vision, or a purpose.

   I. Near the end of his life Joshua offered a stirring challenge to the Israelites. He drew his own precious family and God's nation toward their mission, which was serving the Lord.

  II. Jesus knew that people need a purpose in life. With His last words, He left us with a vision for the world, which is to believe in Jesus, obey Him, teach others, and continue to obey.

III. The first-century disciples were constantly drawing Christians toward this goal, spreading the gospel to all the world.

Conclusion: Without a vision people are apt to wander, caught up in busy work. As a leader, help women set attainable goals or steps so they might realize that which is everlasting. Keep the target before them, and before yourself.

Chapter Nine

DELEGATE

Select from all the people able men, such as fear God, men of truth, hating covetousness; and place such over them to be rulers of thousands, rulers of hundreds, rulers of fifties, and rulers of tens. And let them judge the people at all times. Then it will be that every great matter they shall bring to you, but every small matter they themselves shall judge. So it will be easier for you, for they will bear the burden with you.

—Exodus 18:21-22

As you probably have guessed up to this point with my writing, I love the Old Testament. I am continually drawn to the scarlet thread of God's redemption which begins in Genesis and is woven throughout the Old Testament, coming to fruition in the New Testament. I love to study the geographical areas of the Old Testament, the history of that time. The customs and manners of that era are intriguing. I love its characters: men, women, teens, and children. I love to study the qualities in the men and women of the Old Testament who volunteered to lead God's people, or those who really did not want the job, but it was theirs nonetheless. What qualities made them great? What qualities or actions brought them low?

The Bible, Old and New Testaments, is replete with examples of great leaders who learned how to delegate effectively. For a few moments, please consider with me the lives of Moses, David, and some New Testament examples as well. I truly believe we can and should learn from their experiences which God has so lovingly guarded and preserved through the ages for our benefit (1 Corinthians 10:1–5). The book of Exodus takes its readers through the life experiences of the Israelites as God saved a little baby who grew up to eventually lead His people out of Egyptian captivity. These remarkable chronicles take us on a mad rollercoaster ride, climbing up, up, up, only to fall wildly, then climb up again. Moses, after leading the people through the Red Sea and witnessing the destruction of the army of Pharaoh, fell into an unwelcome role, something between a patriarch/judge and an approachable hero. Neither role seemed to fit the eighty-year-old shepherd. The people came to him with every concern, big or small, until scripture says that "Moses sat to judge the people; and the people stood before Moses from morning until evening" (Exodus 18:13).

Moses' older and wiser father-in-law, Jethro, observed the steady flow and gave some advice to the leader. He told Moses, "The thing that you do is not good." And, in my own words, "Son, you and the people are wearing yourselves out!" Jethro ventured further, telling Moses he should continue to give the people the words of God, the commands, and statutes. But he should

> select from all the people able men, such as fear God, men of truth, hating covetousness; and place such over them to be rulers of thousands, rulers of hundreds, rulers of fifties, and rulers of tens. And let them judge the people at all times. Then it will be that every great matter they shall bring to you, but every small matter they themselves shall judge. So it will be easier for you, for they will bear the burden with you (Exodus 18:21–22).

Jethro's few words of counsel to his son-in-law were priceless pearls of wisdom, which any leader should heed. Moses, a humble man in his dealings with the Israelites, allowed the people to draw more from him than was needed. He was trying to do his job, as well as the job of a hundred others. This obviously did not flow out of arrogance, but a true desire to help others. Leaders today can and do fall into this same trap. Jethro showed him that he could accomplish the same objective by delegating some responsibilities to trustworthy men. He directed Moses to tap into the energy of the talented, good-hearted people of Israel.

A similar experience occurred in the life of David. Most of us remember David's leadership skills as a young man, delivering goods to his brothers who were soldiers in the Israelite camp. The young shepherd, about seventeen, was appalled with the lack of courage among the soldiers. He boldly said that he could, with the help of God, defeat Goliath. King Saul gave him the opportunity to prove his words. With a sling and some smooth stones from a nearby creek, David felled the giant. As readers we marvel at David's faith and his courage as a young man. While this story of David is quite familiar, I wonder if we remember that later in life David came up against another giant. In fact, there were four giants, and the latter story has a very different twist than the former.

After King Saul's death, after David's kindness to Mephibosheth, after the incident with Bathsheba, and after Absolom's death, we read of a much older David who was again at war with the Philistines. David went down with his servants to fight, but this time scripture says, "David grew faint" (2 Samuel 21:15). A mighty giant called Ishbi-Benob, whose bronze spear was three hundred shekels, thought he could kill David. But Abishai "came to his aid and struck the Philistine and killed him" (verse 17).

After this close call, the men came to David and told him that from now on he would not go out to battle with them, "lest you quench the lamp of Israel." His servants very soon faced another giant called Saph, and Sibbechai killed him. Elhanan, a fellow Bethlehemite, killed the third giant, a brother of Goliath, whose spear was like a weaver's beam. There was yet another confrontation with a fourth Philistine giant, one who had six fingers on each hand and six toes on each foot. Jonathan, David's nephew, killed him, but scripture concluded the story saying, "These four were born to the giant in Gath, and fell by the hand of David and by the hand of his servants" (2 Samuel 21:22). David still led his people, but this time he needed help, the aid of friends, servants, and relatives to do God's work. He was a humble man, just as Moses was wrapped in humility, but his strong desire to help the people drove him to take on more than he could physically handle. It almost cost him his life.

As we look to the New Testament model of leadership, Jesus was often found delegating various duties to the twelve apostles. Early in His ministry Jesus called twelve capable men whom He called apostles (Luke 6:12–16). He sent them out, two by two, with specific instructions (Luke 9:1–6). Some time later, as thousands came for healing of body and soul, the disciples became concerned that the day was drawing to a close and the multitude was far from home. They asked Jesus to send the people away so they could buy their own bread. Jesus ignored their request and said, "You give them something to eat" (Luke 9:13). The disciples knew they did not have enough money to buy that much bread. Jesus told them to go and see how many loaves they could find, and a disciple found only five loaves and two fish. Jesus told the people to sit down in groups; He blessed the food and began to break it into pieces. The disciples distributed to each group and after the meal gathered twelve basketfuls of leftover fragments. Jesus put these men to work.

As the early church grew dramatically, it was faced with some difficulty. The Grecian or Hellenistic widows were being neglected in the daily distribution of necessary items. The apostles called the disciples together and told them to "seek out from among you seven men of good reputation, full of the Holy Spirit and wisdom, whom we may appoint over this business" (Acts 6:3). They went on to explain that they must give themselves "continually to prayer and to the ministry of the word." Seven good men were chosen, among them Stephen. Great leaders understand the importance of delegating.

As we lived and worked in Alabama, I worked alongside a young woman, Cathy McGaughy, who directed (with her husband) many of the summertime Family Bible Schools. She delegated numerous jobs, great and small, with success. I learned much as I observed this young woman who strove to involve as many people in the church as possible. We came very close to achieving our one hundred percent participation goal. She gave each person a job to do in their field of expertise, she trusted them to do their best, and she accepted that things might not be done perfectly. She did not have to have her finger in every pie. J. Vernon Jacobs puts it this way:

> As the leader of a group, your success is going to depend, not only upon yourself, but on the cooperation of every person working with you. If they do not cooperate, you will not accomplish anything, no matter how brilliant you may prove to be.

Cathy was—and still is—a marvelous leader who involved others and challenged people to do things they do well. She encouraged them to try new ventures. They felt comfortable doing so—she put them at ease. The reason? They knew Cathy would never barge in and take over if things were not done her way. They knew criticism would not come from her lips. Even if the work was not done as well as she would have done it, she showered praise on her fellow workers. Everyone loves a compliment. She cultivated a fertile basin of creativity within that church. As a result, people blossomed in their labors. Not only do I emulate her skills, I periodically remind myself that I can learn useful things from people half my age and from people twice my age.

As one studies the examples of great leaders from the Old and New Testaments, much can be learned from the lives of these biblical figures. Effective leaders of men and women learned how to delegate. Moses and David were two great leaders who learned the hard way that one man cannot do it all. They were shown how to delegate, they trusted others to do their appointed jobs, and the work of the Lord was completed. Jesus gave each of us a workable pattern of leadership as He labored daily for three years with the twelve, delegating duties and trusting His followers to finish the work. What was true thousands of years ago is still true today: great leaders know how to delegate.

You may be asking, "But what about the risk? What if people let me down? What if I entrust certain duties to others and they betray my trust?" I must be totally honest and admit that these possibilities exist. Indeed, I have experienced that betrayal personally, and the sting that follows. But, as with all endeavors, the mark of success is risk-taking. And the consequences of not delegating are grave. As we have seen in the lives of Moses and David, either the tasks will wear one out, or the strong desire to help God's people will drive one to take on more than is physically possible.

Do you want to cultivate a fertile basin of creativity and trust within the Lord's church? Get to know the people, their strengths and weaknesses. Involve as many as possible in the good works of the church. Tap into the energy and talent that is within each person. Challenge people to do their best and, without hovering or meddling, allow them to complete the work at hand. And when the work or activity is completed, your work as a leader is not finished. Do not forget the last very important ingredient: shower your fellow workers with praise. It has well been said: "Good equippers do like Jesus did it: recruit twelve, graduate eleven, and focus on three."

Questions

1. What events lead up to Moses' near burn-out as a leader?
2. What advice did his father-in-law, Jethro, give him?
3. Relate the events which prompted King David to learn the art of delegation.
4. Was Jesus a leader who delegated responsibilities? Explain.
5. How does it make you feel when you have received a compliment? How important is praise for a job well done?

Outline of *"Delegate"*

Introduction: A good leader recognizes quickly the value of delegating duties. One who chooses another route simply meets with failure. The Bible is replete with examples of great leaders who learned how to delegate effectively.

I. Jethro, Moses' father-in-law, taught him how to select men to help in the judging of the people of Israel.

II. David, in later life, learned how to let people help him accomplish the work of the Lord. It took a united front to defeat four Philistine giants.

III. Jesus delegated many duties to the twelve apostles. The apostles learned this valuable lesson from the Lord. Early in the ministry they delegated to seven men the responsibility of distributing necessities to the Grecian widows.

IV. Cathy McGaughy gave a beautiful example of leadership in action as she tried to enlist as many as possible in VBS. Her goal was to involve one hundred percent and the church was able to reach ninety-five percent.

Conclusion: Know the strengths of the followers and tap into their energy. Get others involved. Trust them to do their best. Finally, don't forget to praise the workers.

Chapter Ten

Don't Be Afraid to Learn

Your hands have made me and fashioned me; give me understanding, that I may learn Your commandments. Those who fear You will be glad when they see me, because I have hoped in Your word.

—Psalm 119:73–74

The responses to the questionnaires that I passed out in preparation for this study on female Christian leadership were remarkable. The women who responded were of different ages—young and old, married and unmarried. Some had small children and others had children who were married. I was intrigued by their answers. Each sheet had only one simple request, "Please list the qualities that are possessed by a female Christian leader." I expected to read list after list of attributes. Instead, I found that most of the women began to chronicle their own lives. They saw themselves as leaders. Do you see yourself as a leader?

One widow, Phoebie, began by writing that as a new Christian at the age of sixteen years old she left home for the first time to live in a nearby town. The first thing she did was find a church home. The elders of that church asked her to teach a young ladies' class. Though young herself, she embraced the opportunity. Continuing, she told of the many opportunities that had been afforded her to lead others. She and others who responded wrote that a leader of women should be open to new opportunities and new ideas, keeping abreast of the world and ideologies. In short, they said a great leader is not afraid to learn.

The respondents wrote that if a great leader is not particularly creative, she tries to learn to be more creative. One way to accomplish this is to surround herself with creative people and learn from them. The leader is well read. Her reading material covers a wide variety of subjects: books and articles about people, fiction, and self-help. Additionally, they said her most important source is God's Word, the preeminent self-help manual. She is ever ready, hungering and thirsting to learn more about God and His plan for humankind. She recognizes her own weaknesses and seeks to improve herself, first spiritually, then emotionally, intellectually, and socially in order to be a well-rounded leader in her home, in the church, and in her community.

The psalmist wrote of his hunger to learn of God: "Your hands have made me and fashioned me; give me understanding that I may *learn* your commandments" (Psalm 119:73). Do you hunger to know more about God? As Jesus walked upon the earth, He encouraged the burdened, "Take my yoke upon you and *learn from Me,* for I am gentle and lowly in heart, and you will find rest for your souls" (Matthew 11:29). Learning is sometimes not easy, especially when our flaws are exposed in the process. Jesus assures us that if we learn from Him, if we emulate His meekness, we will find rest. John recorded Jesus' words as He reminded listeners, "It is written in the prophets, 'And they shall all be taught by God.' Therefore everyone who has heard and *learned* from the Father comes to me" (John 6:45). Learning has its rewards.

After Jesus' ascension, the apostles and disciples continued to learn, and they stressed the importance of learning to those younger preachers who would carry on the work of the Lord for years to come. Paul told the young man, Titus, "Let our people also *learn* to maintain good works, to meet urgent needs, that they may not be unfruitful" (Titus 3:14). He encouraged the young preacher, Timothy, "You must continue in the things which you have *learned* and been assured of, knowing from whom you have *learned* them" (2 Timothy 3:14). Paul exhorted the brothers and sisters at Philippi: "The things which you *learned* and received and heard and saw in me, these do, and the God of peace will be with you" (Philippians 4:9). The Christian can never say, "I know everything I need to know."

In addition to learning more about God each day, the Christian woman should seek to improve in other areas. As human creatures, we all share a basic desire—we treasure our comfort zone. And that zone is not exclusively our home. If you disagree with that statement, please reflect for a moment on your worship experience. When you walk into the building, do you think about where you will sit? Or are you like the majority who always make a path to "their" pew?

With something as basic as where we choose to sit, it is easy to see that we like to be comfortable, and if the place or situation is new, then we create a comfort zone. We like to surround ourselves with people and things that make us feel comfortable. So when someone suggests we step out of our comfort zone and try something new, it is the equivalent of suggesting we try to go to the moon. (Some have actually looked at me as if I were an alien when I suggested trying something new!) But as much as we like the familiar, as leaders we must be willing to learn, and learning many times requires stretching, growing, and becoming a bit uncomfortable in the process.

Are you ready for the challenge? Do want to grow as a leader in your home, in the church, in your community? If so, begin to stretch, begin the process by looking introspectively and asking some critical questions. The following are areas in which each of us should ask ourselves, "Do I need to improve?"

1. *Learning God's Word:* Am I a good student of the Bible? Do I have a proper grasp of the fundamentals? Am I still nourishing myself on the milk when I should be in the meat of the Word?

2. *Learning problem solving skills:* Do I know how to go in meekness and confront an individual who is sinning? Do I know how to lead others to settle disputes quickly and in a Christlike manner? How do I react to conflict? Do I act like a turtle by withdrawing into my shell? Or, like a hornet, do I strike out at those who disturb me?

3. *Learning public speaking skills:* Do I effectively lead and direct others in public settings? Do I overlook my inabilities and at least try to teach or speak to others?

4. *Learning to pray publicly:* Would I lead a prayer at a school function if only women were present? If not, why not? When was the last time I accepted an opportunity to pray with other ladies?

5. *Learning good communication skills:* Do I hesitate to tell people what I am thinking? Am I a good listener? Do I constantly interrupt others during a conversation? Do I monopolize the conversation? Am I too quiet when in public settings? As a leader, do I keep people informed with accurate and up-to-date information?

6. *Learning to be creative:* Do I shy away from service projects because they seem to be for those creative folks? If I recognize that I am a logical, analytical type, do I try to surround myself with creative people and tap into their energy? If I recognize that I am creative, do I share my skills with others who could benefit?

7. *Learning to be flexible:* Does everything always have to be perfect? Can I delegate a good work and trust the person to do her best? Am I constantly looking over

shoulders to see if I can make some corrections? Remember the adage: "If you aren't flexible, you'll break!"

8. *Learning organizational skills:* Am I always losing necessary items? Am I continually late for meetings and worship services? Do I know how to make a list and follow it? Do I need a daily planner? Am I familiar with the use of Post-It notes?

9. *Learning to understand people:* Am I impatient with those around me? Have I taken the time to become familiar with different personality types—introverted, extroverted, self-motivated, analytical, nurturer/caretaker—or different learning styles—the visual learner, the auditory learner, the kinesthetic learner? Do I tend to believe everyone should react the same as I react, or feel the way I feel, or learn the way I learn?

10. *Learning to make the most of personal hygiene, appearance, and personality (the total me):* Do I leave the house without ever glancing at my appearance? Have I ever tried to improve a negative part of my own personality? Do I have a bad temper? Do I tend to gossip? Do I have to be in control all the time?

11. *Learning to be hospitable:* Do I enjoy having people in my home? Do I occasionally meet with friends at a restaurant and enjoy their company?

12. *Learning how to think:* Do I ever seek out new programs that work successfully in other settings? Do I often find myself asking questions (the sign of a good thinker) or do I often find myself having a quick answer for everything (the sign of a know-it-all)?

13. *Learning how to get people to say yes:* Do people run when they see me coming? Do I begin a request with a disclaimer like, "I know you're a busy person, but . . ."? Do I begin a request with a compliment or word of encouragement?

14. *Learning how to step out of my comfort zone:* Do I choose to sit in the same spot during each worship service? Or do I occasionally sit in a new place during worship, enabling me to meet and truly get to know members of my church family?

These are but a few areas in which each of us who desire to be leaders may need to improve. If you feel a bit overwhelmed at first, pick only three areas, and for a time, focus on the three until you feel at ease with your improvement and increased knowledge. Then move on to some other areas, perhaps some which are not listed above, which could help mold you into the leader you want to become. Let us commit to be like my dear Phoebie and challenge ourselves to grow when we are young and single, married with children, married with an empty nest, or widowed. Remember the great leaders of the Bible who recognized their own human inadequacies and learned from God, and from their fellow man. Don't be afraid to learn.

We must never shy away from an impossible situation. When the odds seem least favorable for our success, that is when God can gain the greatest glory.

—author unknown

Questions

1. In what ways do you see yourself as a leader/servant?

2. What steps are you taking to know more about God?

3. What statements did the apostles and other writers of the New Testament make which indicate we should continue to learn?

4. What are some areas in which you need to improve?

Outline of
"Don't Be Afraid to Learn"

Introduction: In the responses to my questionnaire, Pheobie told of the many opportunities to lead others that had been afforded her. She and others wrote that a good leader should not be afraid to learn.

   I. The psalmist wrote of his hunger to learn of God.

  II. Jesus desired that all people should learn from Him.

 III. Paul encouraged young preachers and Christians to continue in their learning.

 IV. A good leader will seek to improve herself in many areas.

Conclusion: Let us commit to grow as leaders. Remember the great leaders of the Bible who recognized their own inadequacies and were not afraid to continue the learning process. Learn of God and learn from your fellow man.

Chapter Eleven

PRAY, PRAY, DON'T EVER STOP PRAYING

> The effective, fervent prayer of a righteous man avails much. Elijah was a man with a nature like ours, and he prayed earnestly that it would not rain; and it did not rain on the land for three years and six months. And he prayed again, and the heaven gave rain, and the earth produced its fruit.
> —James 5:16–18

One simply cannot discuss the role of leaders in the church without talking about prayer. There will come a day when she/he will have problems to which there are no instant solutions. She will eventually be disappointed in others, even herself. Likely she will be thrust into the middle of a confrontation or be asked to mediate in others' disputes. She will likely be tempted to sin as she faces pride, selfishness, gossip, or any myriad of life's enticements. Be assured, Satan is alive and well today. She will face criticism and even though it may be cushioned by the adjective *constructive,* it still hurts. She will experience mountain-top moments as she leads others in their spiritual mountain climbing. She will discover that many times the good far outweighs the difficulties, as is the case with most worthwhile endeavors.

It is a fact, the lows and the highs come with the job. But these feelings are not unique to leaders, nor should we allow them to discourage us. A young mother endures the bloating, the fatigue, and the sorrow in childbirth but promptly forgets these lows when her newborn is placed in her arms. Her heart swells with joy, her tears are tears of joy, and one of her greatest pleasures is sharing those precious moments with her husband, who comforts her and protects her. The same is true in the spiritual realm.

Leaders may have friends who help or comfort through difficult times and there may be someone who shares in her joy, but there is no greater person with whom to share the lows, middles, and highs of your spiritual walk than with the Father who reigns in Heaven. Prayer is a leader's best friend. Prayer gives her the best offensive strategy in doing the will of God. Prayer is also her first line of defense. Prayer should be part of every moment of her life.

Paul put it simply: Pray, pray, don't ever stop praying. (1 Thessalonians 5:17.) Remember the power is not in the leader of the group, but in the Creator of the universe. Prayer helps us recognize that the power is not in me, but in Thee (Philippians 4:13). We trust that God can take our mistakes and turn them into victories, our weaknesses into triumph. (2 Corinthians 12:9). Through prayer we recognize and acknowledge God's will in all we set about to accomplish (1 John 5:14). In prayer all glory and honor is given to God above.

In his *10 Steps to Leadership*, Jacobs recommends the inclusion of these six qualities in the leader's prayer: adoration, confession, thanksgiving, supplication, submission, and fellowship (page 84). So that I could better remember these necessary attributes, I have put them in acrostic form as a memory tool:

P – praise
R – repentance which is acknowledged through confession
A – appreciation or thanksgiving
Y – yielding to God's will
E – entreaty or supplication
R – renewal of fellowship with God

Jesus expressed these characteristics profoundly as He set about to teach the disciples to pray (Luke 11:1–4). His words of praise open the prayer, "hallowed be Your name." He taught that one should ask for forgiveness. In doing so, one acknowledges sin. Though His thanksgiving is not recorded in this prayer, it is found in His prayer as the seventy returned from their evangelistic mission, "I thank You, Father, Lord of heaven and earth, that You have hidden these things from the wise and prudent and revealed them to babes" (Luke 10:21). In the model prayer, as in His other prayers, Jesus openly stated, "Your will be done on earth as it is in heaven." He also taught that we should make supplication to the Father for our needs, "Give us this day our daily bread" and, "Do not lead us into temptation, but deliver us from the evil one." And it is very evident in His first four words, "Our Father in heaven," that he was reaffirming His relationship or fellowship with God the Father.

As Jesus walked upon the earth, He was a man and at the same time He was God. I find it remarkable and a bit difficult to grasp that Jesus had the power to do all things, but He relinquished that right. He did not postpone talking to God until times were rough. We see through the inspired pages that Jesus often stopped His very important, very urgent work, the work He was sent to do, in order to commune with His Father. It appears prayer was as vital to the Son of God as breathing air.

Jesus lifted His voice to the Father as John baptized Him in the wilderness (Luke 3:21). Luke records that Jesus often "withdrew to pray" (Luke 5:16). He prayed before choosing the twelve apostles (Luke 6:12–16). He taught believers to pray for all men, even their enemies (Luke 6:28). He prayed before accomplishing a great miracle and before eating (Luke 9:16). When faced with the knowledge of His impending death, even though Peter, James, and John were near, He needed to talk to His Father (Luke 9:28). During moments of exceeding joy, He offered prayers of thanksgiving (Matthew 11:25). He spoke of the persistent widow, encouraging listeners to be persistent in prayer (Luke 18:1–8). He prayed with the disciples during the last supper (Matthew 26:26–29). He prayed for Himself and His disciples (Luke 22:40–46; John 17). And nearing His death He prayed for those who were spitting on him, those who drove nails into His flesh (Luke 23:34). We often sing that He could have called angels to destroy the world as they were nailing His hands to a tree. Instead, He spoke to His Father.

Jesus' life and the lives of the apostles and believers of the first century point each of us toward the importance of prayer. Following Jesus' resurrection and the birth of the new kingdom on Pentecost, the Lord's church, Luke records that the thousands of new believers "continued steadfastly in the apostles' doctrine and fellowship, in the breaking of bread, and in prayers" (Acts 2:42). Because Lydia and other women were found at the Philippian riverside praying, "the Lord opened her heart to heed the things spoken by Paul" Acts 16:14). Lydia obeyed the gospel and led her household to obedience.

How is your prayer life? Do you do all other things to the neglect of prayer? Or do you concentrate on prayer to the neglect of your Bible study? Remember that any functioning relationship demands communication, and communication is a two-way street; it requires my listening and my speaking. Our relationship with the Lord is no different. It requires my listening to God through a study of His word, and my speaking to God through diligent prayer. If one fails to listen to God by knowing His Word, a dysfunctional relationship will occur, and the same is true if we fail to speak continually to our Father.

A strong, vibrant prayer life helps us, as leaders, focus on the source of our strength and the source of our salvation. We should want to grow in prayer and in other skills which enable us to do the Lord's work, to make a difference in the growth of the kingdom, to make a difference in our communities, and to make a difference in our homes. Do you have a willing heart? Do you have willing hands? Will you lead? If so, we leaders must renew our communication with our Father in Heaven. Prayer should be more than a rescue attempt or a salve for one's guilt. Prayer is vital. Peter, one of God's inspired writers, encouraged each of us to look to the Master, our model of leadership, and to follow His steps (1 Peter 2:21). Though Jesus was divine, His entire life emphasized His own need and our need for communication with the Father. Pray, pray, don't ever stop praying.

Questions

1. What types of problems or discouraging events affect the lives of leaders?

2. Describe some of the highs and lows which are unique to leaders.

3. What does Paul say of prayer in 1 Thessalonians 5:17?

4. On a scale of one-to-ten, describe Jesus' prayer life.

5. On what occasions did Jesus talk to His Father?

6. How did Lydia lead her family to salvation through prayer?

7. With regard to prayer, do I have a functional or dysfunctional relationship with the Father?

Outline of
"Pray, Pray, Don't Ever Stop Praying"

Introduction: Leaders are thrust into every conceivable situation. This may produce emotional highs and lows, but we should not allow these feelings to discourage us. The power source available to all leaders is prayer.

I. Paul put it simply when he said, "Pray, pray, don't ever stop praying." The power is not in the leader of the group, but in the Creator of the universe.

II. An acrostic may help in remembering the qualities needed in prayer.

III. Jesus left a great legacy of prayer. As a leader, He taught believers how to pray. He also lived a life of prayer.

Conclusion: Any functioning relationship demands communication, and communication is a two-way street. It requires my listening and my speaking. Our relationship with the Lord is no different. It requires my listening to God through study of His word and my speaking to God through diligent prayer. A strong prayer life helps us, as leaders, focus on the source of our strength and the source of our salvation.

Chapter Twelve

CONFLICTED OR CONVICTED:
A MODEL OF FEMALE LEADERSHIP

> Do not think in your heart that you will es-
> cape in the king's palace any more than all
> the other Jews. For if you remain completely
> silent at this time, relief and deliverance will
> arise for the Jews from another place, but you
> and your father's house will perish. Yet who
> knows whether you have come to the kingdom
> for such a time as this?
>
> —Esther 4:13–15

There are only two books in the Bible devoted primarily to the lives of women: Ruth and Esther. Though each
narrative contains only a brief account of a particular portion of their lives, the glimpse is fascinating. Ruth's story
reveals a human love unparalleled in scripture, except perhaps that of Hosea. Of course it goes without saying, the
love of Jesus, who was both human and divine, was and is
the greatest love of all. And then there is the book about
the beautiful young woman called Esther, or Hadassah in
Hebrew, whose compelling leadership and courage in her
youth continue to inspire both women and men of all ages.

Esther's story is intriguing. It contains everything of
which a great movie or best-selling novel is made. A powerful king, beautiful women, a good guy who took in an
orphan and averted a planned assassination of the king, a

bad guy with egotism gone awry, revenge, a plot to kill an entire race of people, and an escape that rested solely on the small shoulders of a lovely young woman. Amazing! Esther's cousin, Mordecai, was part of a family which had been captured years earlier under the rule of King Nebuchadnezzar of Babylon. The Babylonian kingdom was eventually overtaken by the Medes and Persians. Under Persian rule the Jews, as well as other conquered nations, were treated with leniency. Many of the Jews had been allowed to return to Jerusalem, but some chose to stay in the land that had become the only home known to them. Esther was probably born in Persia. Scripture says little about her parents except that when they died, Mordecai took the lovely and beautiful Esther as his own daughter (Esther 2:7).

When the king decreed that there would be a national beauty pageant in order to select a new queen, all the fair virgins of the land were gathered to the citadel at Shushan, or Susa. It appears that the young maidens had no choice in the matter. The citadel was a remarkable winter retreat for Persian royalty. Splendor was in abundance, as well as wealth, costly clothes, precious stones, marble, and art. It was a modern, metropolitan hub of the Persian empire.

Esther went to the palace with a charge from Mordecai to keep secret her Jewish lineage. The women were gathered and delivered to the custodian of the women, a eunuch called Hegai. Each woman was given an allowance, but Hegai favored Esther. She was given beauty preparations and the best room in the house, as well as seven maidservants. When all was said and done, Esther won the beauty pageant and King Ahasuerus placed the royal crown on her head proclaiming her to be queen instead of Vashti.

Though Esther no longer lived in his house, Mordecai did not forget his young cousin. Throughout the beauty preparations, which took an entire year, he had gone to the palace daily to inquire of her well being. Even after

Esther was crowned, Mordecai continued to go to the king's gate, which proved providential. One day, he overheard a plot between two fellows who were going to assassinate the king. Mordecai quickly informed Esther, who informed the king. The two assassins were hanged and the account was written in the king's chronicles.

The events quickly shifted to another area in the palace—the king promoted one of his trusted princes. Haman was a manipulative, self-seeking individual who possessed chameleon-like qualities. He knew how to speak words of flattery while in the presence of the king, but struck fear in the hearts of the palace servants. It appears, from all accounts, that he was one who chose any method to climb to the top of the political ladder, including the elimination of those who might appear to be an obstacle in the climbing.

While all those within the palace gates would bow and pay homage to Haman, Mordecai refused to bow to do so. The servants warned him of Haman's wrath, but he revealed to them that he was a Jew and he would not bow down to this man. Did Mordecai make the revelation because Jews were granted a measure of protection under Persian law? Or did he reveal his Jewish heritage to explain why he could not bow down to a *man?* We are left to speculate.

Word travels fast, especially if tattlers are carrying the message. Haman quickly learned of the snub and was filled with wrath. He wanted to kill the insubordinate foreigner immediately, but because of Mordecai's Jewish lineage, he restrained the murderous impulse. Instead, he devised a wicked plan to kill all the Jews who lived throughout the entire kingdom of Persia.

Haman, a man who knew the pull of pride and arrogance, used his manipulative skills to persuade King Ahasuerus to unwittingly sign a decree which would put to death those whose laws were different or those who did not keep the king's commands—in other words, Mordecai and all other Jews under Persian rule.

The day was set. On the thirteenth day of Adar every Jew, both young and old, little children and women, would be annihilated. When Mordecai and the Jews of the provinces learned of the decree, they tore their clothes and cried with a loud and bitter cry. The news that Mordecai was in mourning traveled to Esther. She inquired through a servant to learn why her cousin was in distress.

Mordecai told the servant all that had happened. He gave him a written copy of the decree that he might show it to Esther, and asked her to plead their case before the king. After receiving Mordecai's message, her first response was an excuse, but one might argue that hers was a reason. Esther sent a message back to her cousin explaining that no man or woman could go into the inner court of the king unannounced without the risk of being put to death. If the king held out his golden scepter, the unannounced visitor would live.

Esther's cousin sent one last message to the young queen. He told her she could not expect to escape death just because she was royalty. Mordecai gently advised that if she did not go before the king, help would come for the Jews from another place. But the help might not be soon enough to save Esther. And he added, "Who knows whether you have come to the kingdom for such a time as this?"

Most people, in their youth, do not confront life-and-death situations, let alone the burden of considering the lives of an entire race of people. One can only imagine the weight Mordecai's request put on the heart and mind of young Esther. She must have been deeply conflicted—torn between the desire to continue to live, if but a short while, and the desire to save her cousin and her people. The two desires were seemingly incompatible, but out of the struggle there arose within Esther a precious fruit. As I read the account, I see a young woman who examined her excuse and weighed the cost. No longer conflicted, Esther became convicted. She decided she must try to make a difference, trusting that she would eventually be able to sort through the complicated details.

As a newly born leader, Esther recognized her purpose and the intended goal—the salvation of her people—and she pointed others toward that goal. In true leadership form, Esther went immediately to work delegating important tasks and trusting that the tasks would be completed. She must have believed deeply in the power of prayer because she imposed a fast that would begin with herself and her maids and include all the Jews in the land. With sure and steadfast purpose she communicated this message to the cousin whom she loved as a father. She would go in to see the king, unannounced. Her words of courage and conviction ring loud and clear, "And if I perish, I perish!"

Three days later the beautiful Esther entered the king's court and stood . . . waiting . . . until the king raised his royal scepter, sparing her life. He asked, "What do you wish, Queen Esther? What is your request? It shall be given to you; up to half the kingdom!" Her request was indirect. She invited him and his trusted right-hand man, Haman, to a banquet. A feast? Eating was not foremost on Esther's mind, however. She had a plan. The young queen must have heard the expression: "The way to a man's heart is through his stomach." She had piqued the interest of the king. What could his queen desire that would prompt her to risk her life? She kept the guessing game alive as she ignored the king's question and invited both men to another banquet on the following day.

Haman left the first dinner rejoicing . . . until he saw Mordecai, who refused to bow and tremble before him. He was so filled with murderous rage that he could not enjoy his good fortune as a special guest of the king and queen. His wife and friends advised him to build a gallows, fifty cubits high, and suggest to the king that Mordecai be hanged on it. The unwritten implication was that this Jew would serve as an example to all others of the perils of refusing to honor the king's most favored advisor.

That night the king, suffering from a royal case of insomnia, called for his chronicles to be read before him. The account of Mordecai's earlier help in averting his assassination prompted the king to ask, "What honor or dignity has been bestowed on Mordecai for this?" His servants recalled that nothing had been done, so the king asked for the nearest advisor. As it happened, Haman had come to make his request concerning the gallows and was brought in to the king's chambers. The king asked him, "What shall be done for the man whom the king delights to honor?" Haman, thinking arrogantly that the king was referring to him, advised that a royal robe be brought which the king had worn and a horse which the king had ridden. Let them be brought by the hand of the king's most noble prince and parade this robed man on horseback through the city proclaiming this honor. Ahasuerus liked the suggestion and commanded Haman to do so for Mordecai the Jew. Haman was forced to honor the man he hated. He obeyed the command purely out of duty to the king and went home in mourning.

Meanwhile, Esther prepared the second banquet. The king's eunuchs fetched the noble Prince Haman, and together the king and favored advisor went to dine with the queen. By this time the king's curiosity had been fully aroused. He had offered her up to half his kingdom, yet she still had not made her request. He asked her again, "What is your petition, Queen Esther?" She immediately petitioned the king for her life, and the lives of her people. King Ahasuerus inquired, "Who is he, and where is he, who would dare presume in his heart to do such a thing?" Esther revealed the source of her distress, the wicked Haman. In his wrath, the king ordered Haman hanged on the gallows he had built for Mordecai the Jew.

The danger had not passed, however, for the Jews in Persia. Under Persian rule, a law signed with the king's signet ring could not be revoked. Continuing in leadership, Esther persuaded the king to write a new law allowing her countrymen to defend themselves against any who would seek to assault or destroy her people. More than seventy-five thousand enemies of the Jews were defeated and a holiday was declared on the fourteenth and fifteenth days of the month of Adar to celebrate the day of rest from their enemies. The feast days were to be filled with gladness and the giving of presents to each other and to the poor. Jews continue to this day to celebrate the Feast of Purim, dedicated and confirmed by Queen Esther and her cousin, Mordecai.

Esther's courage and leadership were remarkable for one so young. Though she quickly offered an excuse when first asked to lead, she accepted the role and embraced her goal, the deliverance of all the Jews living in the empire of Persia. She prayed, she planned, she delegated, and she followed through with conviction until salvation was realized. What a woman! For those who desire leadership, Queen Esther's story is a blueprint for success.

Willing Volunteerism
(Larry Sheehy)

The Bible sometimes refers to the people of God in military terminology (Ephesians 6:11–17; 2 Timothy 2:3; et al.). We are the army of the Lord, called into service to do battle with Satan. Our purpose, with Christ as our leader, is to defeat the devil's efforts to lead us and others away from God. There can be no greater or more worthwhile task given to those who serve God.

Historically, people have been inducted into the military either by being drafted, or by volunteering. But in the spiritual army of God, there is no such thing as forced conscription. People willingly choose to become soldiers in the army. They do so out of a desire to serve God and others. They do so with a spirit of joy and thankfulness, rather than one of dread. Oh, there may be a degree of uncertainty. The literal fear of God my help move them. But in every sense of the term, it is a personal, freely made decision. This is the very nature of faith, the basic factor in our response to God's call.

That same spirit of volunteerism continues to characterize the life of God's devoted soldiers the rest of their lives. Someone might object that God gives us commands, which we must obey. This is true, both for those wanting to enter the Lord's army, and for those wishing to continue in His service. But a primary emphasis is the willful choice we make in obedience. "Endure hardship" is as much a command as is "repent and be immersed." Another might point to Paul's reference to our relationship to Christ as "slaves" (Romans 6:16ff). The context, however, shows that spiritual slavery, "whether . . . to sin, which leads to death, or to obedience, which leads to righteousness," is a willing slavery, one in which we offer ourselves as slaves to our chosen master.

Because of the volunteer nature of the army of God, it naturally follows that without a spirit of willing volunteerism—is there any other kind?—the army will be hampered in its efforts to move forward. Soldiers in human armies can be forced to move, if necessary. God's troops move voluntarily, even while under the command of Jehovah. This is why it is so important for us to be willing to follow where Jesus leads in the fight against Satan.

When soldiers rebel against authority or insist on a selfish pursuit of personal goals, the army of God is hampered and the devil wins. When we are unwilling to volunteer our resources and use them in the service of our King, we show our contempt for the glory of God and the souls of others.

The final victory of God over Satan has been foreseen. It is sure. But our part in it, and that of those we influence, depends to a large extent on our willingness to volunteer ourselves in faithful service in God's army.

—Statesboro, Georgia

Questions

1. How many books in the Bible are devoted primarily to the lives of women?

2. When Esther's parents died, who adopted her?

3. What choice did Esther have with regard to participating in the beauty pageant requested by the king?

4. What was Mordecai's charge to Esther as she left his home?

5. Describe the beauty preparations given to the pageant contestants.

6. In what way did Mordecai express continued concern for Esther?

7. How did Mordecai save the king's life? How was his act acknowledged?

8. Describe the king's trusted prince, Haman.

9. How did Haman come to know Mordecai?

10. How did Haman plan to take revenge on Mordecai?

11. After Mordecai revealed to Esther the wicked plan, what emotions do you believe she might have experienced?

12. Describe Esther's plan to expose Haman's wickedness.

13. What was the king's response when he learned of Haman's plot?

14. What great feast began to be celebrated by the Jews in order to remember the courageous queen of Persia?

Outline of
"Conflicted or Convicted:
A Model of Female Leadership"

Introduction: There are only two books in the Bible devoted primarily to the lives of women: Ruth and Esther. Esther's story is an amazing revelation of leadership in action.

I. Esther lived in the house of Mordecai.

II. Following the king's beauty pageant, Esther was chosen as the new queen.

III. Mordecai saved the life of the king, but remained unrecognized for this brave act.

IV. After Mordecai insulted the chief prince, Haman, the Jews in Persia faced destruction plotted by the wicked prince.

V. Esther learned of the plot and put her own plan into action to expose Haman.

VI. When the king learned of the plan to kill all the Jews, he put Haman to death and rewarded Esther and Mordecai.

Conclusion: Esther's courage and leadership were remarkable for one so young. Though she quickly offered an excuse when first asked to lead, she embraced her goal, the deliverance of all the Jews living in Persia. She prayed, she planned, she delegated and she followed through with conviction until salvation was realized.

Chapter Thirteen

OUR CROWN OF REJOICING!

For what is our hope, or joy, or crown of rejoicing? Is it not even you in the presence of our
Lord Jesus Christ at His coming? For you are
our glory and joy.

—1 Thessalonians 2:19–20

Looking back now, as I began this study on female leadership, I approached the subject tentatively, assuming that
there was little to uncover that had not already been written, discussed, hashed, and rehashed. I began the study
perusing God's word for His wisdom and counsel, but I tried
to find outside material as well, which would aid my study.
And while much has been written on the role of women—
wives, motherhood, and such like—I was surprised to find
very little on the topic of female leadership outside of an
occasional chapter in a ladies' class book, or a book which
dealt primarily with female submission. The two words *female* and *leadership* rarely were found together.

I remember going to the local Christian bookstore which
houses a large selection of books and helps for teachers
and ministers of various faiths and practices. Helpless, I
asked a clerk, "Could you direct me toward books about
female leadership in the church?" The lady immediately
took on a blank expression. I got the distinct impression
she might have wondered if she were dealing with a femi-

nist Christian. There were several good books directed toward men, but none for women. I faced sheer frustration in my search for literature based solely on female leadership. My focus returned to the scripture. And, as always is the case, my answers were found in God's Word.

The more I studied, the more I found female leadership in every nook and cranny. I saw countless women of the Old Testament who led quietly, yet powerfully. The New Testament revealed women, almost innumerable, who were constantly at the forefront in God's beautiful scheme of redemption. As I pondered their lives, I saw women very active in the role of the birth and development of the young Savior—Mary, Elizabeth, and the lesser known prophetess, Anna. These three represented women of all ages—young, middle-aged, and aged. Each played a vital role in pointing the world to its Redeemer.

The woman at the well, the woman taken in adultery, Mary Magdalene, and other women gave Jesus an opportunity to display His grace and love even before the sacrifice of His life. When Jesus' closest advisors and friends forsook Him, women led the way following Him to the cross (Luke 23:27). Women led the way to the tomb. On the morning of His resurrection, women went to minister to His lifeless body, but returned and announced the news that the tomb was empty, news that even today brings salvation (Luke 24:10). And, as can be seen in Acts 1, women led quietly as a new kingdom, the church, was ushered into the world. No doubt about it, women are leaders.

These New Testament examples of female leaders, in addition to the examples in previous chapters, both male and female, have crafted a unique picture of leadership. Reflections of women who have had a profound influence on my life, and wisdom gleaned from books and articles designed with men in mind, have also helped me to understand the role of female leadership. They helped me realize that leadership is not dependent on an outgoing personality, or having an active supportive husband, or being a particular age, or possessing beauty and grace—thank you, Lord.

The study helped me to realize that understanding leadership within divine guidelines is essential. Jesus led in the path of submission as He yielded to His Father saying, "Not my will, but yours be done." I learned that the two words *female* and *leadership* do, in fact, go together.

King Saul taught me that refusing to do things God's way reaps a harvest of misery. And in contrast I learned of David, as a young man, who displayed a heart that was attractive to the Lord. Doing things God's way instead of my way is the very heart of salvation.

Being a spiritual, holy leader is a must. I cannot hope to fill someone else's spiritual cup if my own cup is empty. I learned the importance of studying the life of the greatest leader the world has ever known, Jesus Christ, who was first and foremost a servant in shepherd's clothing.

The lives of Moses and Gideon taught me that I must examine my excuses. Jesus and the apostle Paul taught me how to reframe an unpleasant event or situation and put a positive twist on life. Understanding how God despised murmuring and complaining helps me know better how to please Him and involve others.

Joshua and Jesus gave patterns of leadership which help me (and those I lead) to focus on a vision, a world-wide vision. Moses and David taught me that everything does not depend on one person. Jesus taught through example the power of tapping into the strengths and energies of those around me. One who learns how to be a servant of Christ and continues to serve as a leader yields a bountiful harvest.

The knowledge that one does not have to be perfect and that great leaders should be open to learning has the ability to draw out the absolute best in each of us. I learned through Jesus' example that prayer is a leader's first line of defense and her best offense. Prayer should be an integral part of every moment of her life.

And finally, Esther was able to show me the attributes of leadership working in harmony toward a successful end—a perfect model of female leadership. She possessed a willing heart and willing hands. She was willing to lead in the salvation of her people in Persia.

It is my sincere prayer that these examples and thoughts have helped you as well. If this study has enlightened you, or in any way inspired you to see yourself as a leader, then God be praised! For you are precious in His sight and, in truth, we all lead others. Some are leading down the path of materialism, apathy, or outright sin, while others choose to lead souls in the path of righteousness. The question is simple: do you have a willing heart, do you have willing hands, are you willing to lead others to see and know Jesus? If so, this study of female leadership has been fruitful. And, as Paul expressed his devotion to the brothers and sisters in Christ who were obediently leading in the ministry at Thessalonica, I, too, express my devotion to you, sweet sisters, for you are our hope, our glory, and our crown of rejoicing!

Looking Inward

1. Do I see myself as a leader?

2. Do I allow misconceptions to shape my image of a female leader?

3. Do I practice female leadership within divine guidelines?

4. Do I seek to do things God's way instead of my way?

5. Do I occasionally pause to refill my spiritual cup? If so, am I tempted by Satan to do more than pause; am I tempted to quit?

6. Do I seek opportunities to serve others?

7. Have I examined my excuses for not stepping into visible leadership positions?

8. Do I see the good in others? Do I see the good that can come out of unpleasant events or situations?

9. Do I regularly call to attention the vision that was given to us by the Lord?

10. Do I seek to involve as many as possible in the work of the Lord?

11. Am I willing to stretch, to grow, to be open to learning?

12. On a scale of one-to-ten, how do I rate my prayer life?

13. What am I leaving this generation? What am I passing on to my family? In years to come, how will I be remembered by the church and my community?

Outline of *"Our Crown of Rejoicing!"*

Introduction: I began this study of female leadership tentatively, assuming that there was little to uncover that had not already been written. However, I was startled to find, even in a Christian bookstore, that very little had been written on this topic. The two words *female* and *leadership* rarely were found together. My focus returned to the scripture where I found female leadership in every nook and cranny.

I. The Old and New Testament examples of female leaders have crafted a unique picture of leadership which helps one realize that leadership is not dependent on an outgoing personality, having an active supportive husband, being a particular age, or beauty and grace.

II. The words *female* and *leadership* are not like oil and water. The two do go together.

III. Understanding leadership within divine guidelines is essential.

IV. Examples from scripture have taught that doing things God's way is the very heart of salvation.

V. One cannot hope to fill another person's spiritual cup if one's own cup is empty.

VI. Service in leadership is best seen in the life of Jesus, a servant in shepherd's clothing.

VII. The lives of Gideon and Moses teach that excuses must be examined.

VIII. Jesus and Paul teach how to reframe an unpleasant event or situation and maintain a positve outlook.

IX. Joshua and Jesus gave patterns of leadership which help all leaders focus on world-wide vision.

X. The leader does not have to be perfect and should be open to learning.

XI. Prayer is a leader's first line of defense and her best offense.

XII. Esther revealed a beautiful picture of the attributes of leadership working in harmony toward a successful end. She is a perfect model of female leadership.

Conclusion: It is my prayer that this study has enlightened you and inspired you to see yourself as a leader. Ask yourself three simple questions. Do you have a willing heart, do you have willing hands, are you willing to lead others to see and know Jesus? If so, this study has been fruitful. Like Paul, I express my devotion to you, *for you are our hope, our glory, and our crown of rejoicing.*

WORKS CITED

1. Robert D. Dale, *To Dream Again*, Nashville Tennessee: Broadman Press, 1981.

2. J. Vernon Jacobs, *10 Steps to Leadership,* Cincinnati, Ohio: The Standard Publishing Foundation, 1956.

3. John Maxwell, *Developing the Leader Within You*, Nashville, Tennessee: Thomas Nelson Publishers, 1993.